hamlyn cookery club

Easy
pasta

hamlyn cookery club

Easy
pasta

First published in 1999 by Hamlyn
an imprint of Octopus Publishing Group
2–4 Heron Quays
London E14 4JP

British Library Cataloguing-in-Publication Data
A catalogue record for this book is available from the
British Library.

ISBN 0 600 59908 6

Printed in China

Publishing Director: Laura Bamford
Creative Director: Keith Martin
Design Manager: Bryan Dunn
Designer: Jo Tapper
Jacket Photography: Sean Myers
Picture Researchers: Christine Junemann and Stevie Moe
Senior Production Controller: Katherine Hockley

Notes

1 Both metric and imperial measurements have been given in
all recipes. Use one set of measurements only and not a
mixture of both.

2 Standard level spoon measurements are used in all recipes.
1 tablespoon = one 15 ml spoon
1 teaspoon = one 5 ml spoon

3 Eggs should be medium unless otherwise stated.

4 Milk should be full fat unless otherwise stated.

5 Fresh herbs should be used unless otherwise stated.
If unavailable use dried herbs as an alternative but halve the
quantities stated.

6 Pepper should be freshly ground black pepper unless
otherwise stated.

7 Ovens should be preheated to the specified temperature
– if using a fan-assisted oven, follow the manufacturer's
instructions for adjusting the time and temperature.

8 Measurements for canned food have been given as a
standard metric equivalent.

Contents

Introduction

Pasta is quick and easy to prepare as well as being inexpensive, so it is an ideal storecupboard ingredient. It is made from wheat starch, in the case of the Italian varieties this is hard durum wheat, a wheat rich in protein, vitamins and minerals. Pasta is made up mainly of carbohydrate with virtually no fat so it is filling without being high in calories. Allow between 50–125 g (2–4 oz) per person for both dried and fresh pasta. The amount depends on whether it is to be served as a starter or a main course and on how substantial the accompanying sauce is.

Dried Pasta There are hundreds of types of dried pasta available all of which have a long shelf life. Try to choose a dried pasta made from hard durum wheat semolina (*semola di grano duro*), pasta made from a softer, cheaper wheat is less nutritious and more difficult to cook. Pasta is also available in different colours. Most pasta is pale yellow, made from flour and water. If it is a darker yellow this usually means that eggs have been added (*all'uovo*). Green pasta (*pasta verde*) is flavoured with spinach; light red pasta (*pasta rosso*) is flavoured with tomatoes. Wholewheat and buckwheat pasta are brown in colour. Most dried pasta is cooked for between 8–12 minutes for unfilled pasta and about 15 minutes for filled, but always check the packet instructions as different brands do have different cooking times. Wholewheat pasta is higher in fibre than plain pasta and may absorb more water during cooking, so do check it frequently.

Fresh Pasta There are fewer types of fresh pasta available than dried but they are interchangeable with the dried varieties and their nutritional value is the same. Fresh pasta is lighter in texture than dried. Fresh pasta has a relatively short shelf life: 2–4 days in the refrigerator. Fresh pasta takes a much shorter time to cook than dried, usually only 2–3 minutes for unfilled and 8–10 minutes for filled, and it rises to the surface of the boiling water when ready. Most of the recipes in this book use dried pasta but some recipes for making your own fresh pasta are included.

Cooking Pasta Use plenty of water, at least 750 ml (1¼ pints) for every 125 g (4 oz) pasta, and use a large pan. Bring the water to a fast rolling boil. Add salt (this can be omitted if you prefer) and sometimes a little oil is added to separate the pasta and prevent it sticking. Give the pasta a stir, increase the heat and bring back to the boil. Reduce the heat so the water is kept at a rolling boil. Calculate the cooking time from this moment. Keep the pan uncovered and stir the pasta occasionally. Cook for the length of time instructed on the packet. Times though can vary according to the age of the pasta, the quantity of water, the size of the pan and the amount of heat. It is easy to overcook pasta and the best way to judge if it is cooked is to taste it. The Italians say pasta is ready to eat when it is *al dente* which literally means 'firm to the bite'. It should be tender with a slight resistance. As soon as the pasta is ready drain it into a colander or large sieve and shake to remove as much water as possible. Serve the pasta immediately so that it does not become overcooked and soggy.

This chart describes the shape of some of the most common Italian pastas:

PASTA	SHAPE	PASTA	SHAPE
Bucatini	Thick, tubular spaghetti	**Orecchiette**	Small, round ear shaped
Cannelloni	Large hollow tubes	**Orzo**	Very small, rice shaped
Cappelli d'angelo	Long very thin vermicelli, 'angels hair'	**Paglia e Fieno**	Flat ribbon noodles (spinach and egg), coiled into nests
Cappelletti	Small stuffed hats	**Pappardelle**	Wide pasta noodles
Chitarra	Square-shaped spaghetti	**Pastina**	Tiny pasta shapes
Conchiglie	Shells, the size may vary	**Penne**	Short, tubular quills, with angled ends
Farfalle	Bows	**Ravioli**	Filled (round or square) small shapes, sometimes with serrated or fluted edges
Farfallini	Very small bows		
Fettuccine	Long, flat ribbon noodles, often coiled into nests		
Fusilli	Twists, spirals, or coils, long or short	**Rigatoni**	Short-cut, ridged tubes
Lasagne	Flat, rectangular or square sheets, sometimes ridged or with crinkled edges	**Rotelle**	Cartwheels, also called '*ruote*'
Linguine	Thin, flat ribbon noodles	**Spaghetti**	Long, thin strings
		Spaghettini	Long, very thin strings
Lumache	Snails	**Tagliatelle**	Flat, ribbon noodles
Maccheroni	Thick, long and hollow tubes	**Tortellini**	Small stuffed 'navels'
		Tortelloni	Large stuffed 'navels'
Manicotte	Large tubes like cannelloni	**Trenette**	Narrow, flat ribbons
		Vermicelli	Thin pasta strands

Fresh Pasta

Homemade Egg Pasta

500 g (1 lb) plain white or wholemeal flour
2 large eggs
1 teaspoon oil
½ teaspoon salt
3–4 tablespoons water (approximately)

Sift the flour into a heap on a work surface and make a well in the centre. Put the eggs, oil and salt into the well and mix together with your fingers. Gradually work in the flour to form a crumbly dough, adding a little water as necessary. Knead for 10 minutes, until smooth and elastic. Cover and leave to rest for 1 hour.

Roll out the dough on a lightly floured surface, first in one direction and then in the other, continuing until the pasta is paper thin. Shape and use as required.

Makes 500 g (1 lb) quantity

Variation:
Pasta Verde (Green Pasta)
Follow the above recipe, adding 125 g (4 oz) cooked sieved spinach (weighed after having been squeezed very dry) with the eggs but reducing the flour to 375 g (12 oz) and omitting the water.

Shaping Pasta

Stuffed Pasta: The dough should be used immediately, without drying.
Flat and Ribbon Pasta: Dust the dough lightly with the flour and leave to dry for 15–20 minutes, but do not allow to become brittle. Cut flat pasta shapes and roll ribbon pasta into a loose Swiss roll and cut across into strips.

Cooking Pasta

Homemade Pasta: Put the pasta into a large pan containing 2.5–2.75 litres (4–5 pints) fast boiling water and 1½ teaspoons salt. Stir well, then boil steadily, uncovered, for 3–5 minutes until al dente. Test frequently to avoid overcooking, as pasta continues to soften until you eat it. The moment it is done, tip the pasta into a colander, drain thoroughly and serve immediately.
Manufactured Pasta: As above, but follow the packet instructions because cooking times are longer for manufactured pastas and vary considerably for different shapes and brands.

Quantities:

Allow 75–125 g (3–4 oz) pasta per person for a main course, 50 g (2 oz) for a starter.

right: ravioli with ragu

Ravioli with Ragu

Pasta:
1½ x recipe quantity Homemade Egg Pasta (see left)
75 g (3 oz) Pecorino cheese, grated, to serve
Filling:
325 g (11 oz) Pecorino cheese, grated
425 g (14 oz) fresh spinach, cooked, well drained and chopped
2 eggs, beaten
pinch of saffron powder
salt and pepper
Ragu:
3 tablespoons olive oil
1 onion, chopped
125 g (4 oz) fatty bacon or belly pork, chopped
250 g (8 oz) minced veal
1 tablespoon chopped parsley
6 basil leaves, chopped
625 g (1¼ lb) tomatoes, skinned and mashed

Make the pasta and leave to stand for about 1 hour.

Meanwhile, make the filling: put the cheese, spinach, half the beaten egg and the saffron in a bowl. Season with salt and pepper to taste and mix thoroughly.

Flatten the dough with a rolling pin and roll out to a paper-thin sheet. Put heaped teaspoonsful of

the filling over one half of the dough at regular intervals, about 5 cm (2 inches) apart.

Brush the other half of the dough with the remaining egg and place loosely over the filling. Press the pasta firmly between the filling to seal. Cut between the filling to make small squares of ravioli, using a tooth-edged rotary cutter. Place the squares in a single layer on a cloth sprinkled with flour, and leave to dry for about 1 hour.

Meanwhile, make the ragu: heat the oil in a heavy pan, add the onion and bacon and fry gently for 5 minutes. Add the veal, parsley and basil and cook for 10 minutes. Add the tomatoes and salt and pepper to taste. Simmer for 1 hour, adding a little warm water as necessary if the sauce is too thick.

Cook the ravioli in plenty of boiling salted water for 5 minutes or until they rise to the surface. Remove from the pan with a slotted spoon and pile into a warmed serving dish. Pour over the ragu and sprinkle with the grated Pecorino. Serve immediately.

Serves 4

Pasta Roulade

Salsiccia a metro is a long thin, spiced sausage traditionally sold in Italy in one long piece. If it is unavailable, substitute another spicy Italian sausage.

Filling:
40 g (1½ oz) butter
625 g (1¼ lb) calf's liver, chopped
150 g (5 oz) pork loin, chopped
250 g (8 oz) salsiccia a metro, chopped
1 kg (2 lb) fresh spinach

50 g (2 oz) mushrooms, chopped
150 g (5 oz) Parmesan cheese, grated
salt and pepper

Pasta:
325 g (11 oz) plain flour
pinch of salt
3 eggs, beaten

To finish:

25 g (1 oz) Parmesan cheese, grated

65 g (2½ oz) butter, melted

To make the filling: melt the butter in a heavy pan, add the calf's liver, pork and sausage and fry gently for 8 minutes. Cook the spinach in a separate pan, until wilted. Drain thoroughly. Drain the meat, then mince it with the spinach. Add the mushrooms, Parmesan and salt and pepper to taste. Mix well.

To make the pasta: sift the flour and salt on to a work surface and make a well in the centre. Add the eggs and mix to a smooth dough.

Flatten the dough with a rolling pin and roll out to a rectangular sheet, about 3 mm (⅛ inch) thick. Spread the filling over the dough, leaving a 3 cm (1¼ inch) border around the edges. Roll up the dough as for a Swiss roll. Wrap in a piece of muslin and secure the ends with thin string.

Place the roll in a long, narrow flameproof casserole and cover with lightly salted cold water. Bring to the boil, lower the heat and simmer for 20 minutes. Remove the casserole from the heat, and leave the roll to cool in the water.

Remove the muslin and cut the roulade into 1.5 cm (¾ inch) thick slices. Place the slices in a buttered ovenproof dish. Sprinkle with the Parmesan and butter. Place under a preheated hot grill for 5 minutes, then serve immediately.

Serves 6

Lasagne with Ragu

Ragu:

3–4 tablespoons olive oil

50 g (2 oz) butter

1 onion, chopped

375 g (12 oz) minced beef

125 g (4 oz) raw ham or bacon, diced

4 tablespoons white wine

4 tomatoes, skinned and chopped

pinch of grated nutmeg

375 g (12 oz) calf's sweetbreads

salt and pepper

Pasta:

425 g (14 oz) plain flour

pinch of salt

150 g (5 oz) semolina

4 eggs, beaten

50 g (2 oz) lard

3–4 tablespoons white wine

To finish:

125 g (4 oz) Parmesan cheese, grated

50–75 g (2–3 oz) Mozzarella cheese

50 g (2 oz) butter, melted

To make the ragu: heat the oil and butter in a heavy pan, add the onion and fry gently for 5 minutes until golden. Add the beef and ham and cook, stirring, over a moderate heat for 10 minutes. Add the wine, tomatoes, nutmeg and salt and pepper to taste, then lower the heat and simmer for 1 hour.

Meanwhile, cook the sweetbreads in boiling water for 10 minutes, then drain and cut into cubes. Add to the ragu and cook for 5 minutes.

To make the pasta: sift the flour

and salt on to a work surface, stir in the semolina and make a well in the centre. Add the eggs, lard and wine and mix to a smooth dough. Shape into a ball, wrap in a damp cloth and leave to stand for about 30 minutes.

Flatten the dough with a rolling pin and roll into a thin sheet. Cut into lasagne strips, about 10 cm (4 inches) long. Cook the lasagne in plenty of boiling salted water for 6–7 minutes until al dente; drain thoroughly.

Put a layer of lasagne in the bottom of a buttered deep ovenproof dish. Cover with a layer of sauce, then sprinkle with Parmesan and top with a few slices of Mozzarella. Continue these layers until all the ingredients are used, finishing with a layer of cheese. Drizzle over the melted butter. Bake in a preheated oven, 200°C (400°F), Gas Mark 6, for 20 minutes. Serve immediately.

Serves 6

left: pasta roulade

Pasta Sauces

Pesto

This is the basil sauce, as made in Genoa, that is also found in and around Nice and in Provence. In Italy it is made with a mixture of cheeses: half Parmesan and half Sardo, a hard cheese from Sardinia. Since Sardo is not always available in this country, all Parmesan may be used instead.

15 g (½ oz) basil, leaves only
1 garlic clove, chopped
pinch of salt
50 g (2 oz) pine kernels
4 tablespoons grated Parmesan
  cheese
6 tablespoons olive oil
sprigs of basil, to garnish

Put the basil into a food processor or blender and process until finely chopped. Add the garlic, salt, pine kernels and Parmesan and process until reduced to a smooth paste.

Tip the paste into a mortar or heavy bowl, then gradually beat in the olive oil, using either a pestle or heavy wooden spoon. Serve the pesto spooned over pasta, and garnished with a sprig of basil.

Serves 4

Green Tuna Sauce

200 g (7 oz) can tuna in oil, drained
3 anchovy fillets
40 g (1½ oz) chopped parsley
freshly ground white pepper
250 ml (8 fl oz) olive oil
  (approximately)

Put the tuna and anchovy fillets into a blender or food processor. Add the parsley and some pepper. Pour in enough of the oil to make the sauce smooth.

Blend the sauce for 1 minute and serve as much as desired with freshly cooked pasta shells. The rest can be kept for future use.

Serves 4

Italian Vegetable Sauce

A useful sauce to make when summer vegetables are plentiful. This sauce is good just with plain boiled pasta, but is also useful for layering pasta before baking, or for replacing tomato sauce.

1 tablespoon oil
1 onion, finely chopped
1 red pepper, deseeded and finely chopped
1 yellow pepper, deseeded and finely chopped
2 celery sticks, finely chopped
1 courgette, finely chopped
4 tomatoes, skinned, deseeded and chopped
250 g (8 oz) spinach leaves, chopped
150 ml (¼ pint) vegetable stock or water
1 teaspoon caster sugar
salt and pepper

Heat the oil in a large saucepan, add the onion, peppers, celery and courgette and cook for 2 minutes until almost tender.

Stir in the tomatoes, spinach, stock or water, sugar and season with salt and pepper. Bring to the boil and cook for 10 minutes until the sauce has reduced and is thick.

Serves 4

left: green tuna sauce
right: herby tomato sauce

Herby Tomato Sauce

2 tablespoons olive oil
1 large onion, chopped
2 large garlic cloves, crushed
2 x 425 g (14 oz) cans tomatoes, roughly chopped
1 small bay leaf
1 tablespoon chopped fresh lovage or ½ tablespoon dried lovage
1 tablespoon chopped fresh marjoram or ½ tablespoon dried oregano
1 tablespoon chopped fresh thyme or ½ tablespoon dried thyme
1½ teaspoons sugar
salt and pepper
sprig of thyme, to garnish

Heat the oil in a large saucepan, add the onion and cook gently for about 10 minutes until soft but not browned. Add the garlic and cook for a further 2 minutes.

Add the tomatoes, herbs and seasonings. Bring to the boil, lower the heat and simmer, half-covered, for 1 hour, stirring occasionally.

Remove and discard the bay leaf. Taste and adjust the seasoning if necessary. Leave the sauce to cool for a few minutes, then purée briefly in a food processor or blender, or pass through a sieve, and serve with pasta, garnished with a thyme sprig.

Serves 4

Variation:
Fresh tomatoes, when plentiful and cheap, may be substituted for canned. Use 1 kg (2 lb) fresh tomatoes, skinned and roughly chopped. Flavour the sauce with 1½ tablespoons tomato purée.

13

Fresh Tomato Sauce

1 tablespoon olive oil
1 celery stick, chopped
1 carrot, chopped
2 onions, chopped
2 garlic cloves, crushed
1 kg (2 lb) large ripe tomatoes,
 quartered
2 teaspoons caster sugar
2 tablespoons chopped basil
salt and pepper

Heat the oil in a medium saucepan, add the celery, carrot, onions and garlic. Cook gently for 3 minutes until tender.

Stir in the tomatoes, sugar, basil and season with salt and pepper to taste. Bring to the boil, reduce the heat and cover the saucepan with a lid.

Cook gently for 30 minutes, then place in a blender and process until the sauce is smooth

Serves 4–6

Serving idea:
Make this sauce in large quantities when tomatoes are in season and freeze it in small portions. Serve it hot with spaghetti, tagliatelle or pasta shapes.

Bolognese Sauce

This is always a handy sauce to make in quantity and freeze. An ideal partner for spaghetti as well as a base for lasagne.

1 tablespoon vegetable oil
50 g (2 oz) bacon, derinded and
 chopped, or Prosciutto, chopped
1 onion, finely chopped
1 garlic clove, crushed
2 celery sticks, finely chopped
1 carrot, finely chopped
125 g (4 oz) button mushrooms,
 finely chopped
250 g (8 oz) minced beef
4 large ripe tomatoes, skinned,
 deseeded and chopped
2 tablespoons tomato purée
150 ml (¼ pint) red wine
150 ml (¼ pint) beef or vegetable
 stock
1 teaspoon caster sugar
1 bay leaf
salt and pepper

Heat the oil in a saucepan, add the bacon or Prosciutto, onion, garlic, celery, carrot and mushrooms.

Cook rapidly for 2 minutes, stir in the beef and cook until brown. Add the tomatoes, tomato purée, wine, stock, sugar, bay leaf and season.

Bring to the boil, reduce the heat and cover the saucepan with a lid. Cook gently for 45–50 minutes, giving an occasional stir.

Serves 4

Quick Tomato Sauce

1 tablespoon olive oil
2 onions, finely chopped
2 garlic cloves, crushed
2 x 425 g (14 oz) cans chopped
 tomatoes
2 teaspoons caster sugar
½ teaspoon Worcestershire sauce
 (optional)
2 tablespoons chopped fresh or
 1 tablespoon dried basil
salt and pepper

Heat the oil in a medium saucepan. Add the onions and cook gently for 5–6 minutes or until tender.

Stir in the garlic, tomatoes, sugar, Worcestershire sauce, if using, basil and season with salt and pepper to taste. Bring to the boil and cook rapidly for about 5 minutes, or until the sauce has thickened.

Serves 4–6

Serving idea:
Serve this tomato sauce with all varieties of pasta, sprinkled with Parmesan cheese and garnished with basil.

right: fresh tomato sauce, bolognese sauce, quick tomato sauce

Fresh Coriander and Walnut Sauce

1 tablespoon olive oil

50 ml (2 fl oz) double or whipping cream

25 g (1 oz) Cheddar cheese, finely grated

25 g (1 oz) walnuts, finely chopped

25 g (1 oz) coriander, finely chopped

salt and pepper

sprig of coriander, to garnish

Place the olive oil and cream in a bowl and add the cheese, walnuts, coriander, salt and pepper. Mix well together.

Place 125 g (4 oz) cooked pasta twists on a hot dish, pour the sauce on top and mix together. Garnish with the coriander.

This sauce will keep for 1–2 days in a covered container in the refrigerator.

Serves 4

above: fresh coriander and walnut sauce

Penne with Spicy Olive Sauce

500 g (1 lb) penne

125 ml (4 fl oz) olive oil

½ teaspoon ground ginger

generous pinch of grated nutmeg

1 garlic clove, crushed

3 tablespoons capers

75 g (3 oz) pitted black olives, sliced

2 tablespoons chopped fresh parsley

salt and pepper

sprigs of basil, to garnish

Cook the penne in boiling salted water for 10–12 minutes or according to the packet instructions, until al dente. Drain thoroughly.

Return the cooked penne to the pan, together with the oil, ginger, nutmeg, pepper, garlic, capers, olives and parsley. Stir over a gentle heat for 1–2 minutes. Serve immediately, garnished with basil sprigs.

Serves 4

Seafood Sauce

50 g (2 oz) butter or margarine
1 onion, finely chopped
1 garlic clove, crushed
50 g (2 oz) plain flour
450 ml (¾ pint) vegetable stock
150 ml (¼ pint) white wine
125 g (4 oz) halibut, cubed
6 scallops, cut into quarters
50 g (2 oz) canned or frozen mussels
125 g (4 oz) cooked peeled prawns
1 tablespoon chopped marjoram
150 ml (¼ pint) single cream
salt and pepper

Melt the butter or margarine in a medium saucepan, add the onion and garlic, and cook gently for 2 minutes.

Stir in the flour and cook for 1 minute. Gradually add the stock and the wine, stirring continuously, and bring to the boil.

Reduce the heat and stir in the halibut and scallops and cook gently for 2–3 minutes.

Stir in the mussels, prawns and marjoram and some salt and pepper and heat gently for 1 minute.

Just before serving, add the cream and heat through.

Serves 4

Variations:

Replace the mussels and scallops with crab or lobster for a change in flavour, or serve liquidized as a creamy soup.

Mix cooked pasta shapes into the sauce, sprinkle with cheese and grill for a quick supper dish.

Sauce alla Amatriciana

This delicious sauce originates from the Abruzzi region of Italy; a traditional country sauce, it makes a tasty accompaniment to most types of pasta. It is particularly well suited to tubular varieties, such as rigatoni, macaroni or penne.

1 tablespoon sunflower or
  olive oil
75 g (3 oz) lean, unsmoked bacon,
  derinded and diced
1 small onion, finely chopped
1 canned pimiento, chopped
375 g (12 oz) fresh tomatoes, skinned
  and chopped
375 g (12 oz) pasta
salt and pepper

To garnish:

grated Parmesan or Pecorino cheese
sprig of fresh coriander

Heat the oil in a heavy pan, add the bacon and fry gently for 5 minutes until golden. Remove with a slotted spoon, put on one side and keep hot.

In the same pan, fry the onion until transparent, then add the pimiento, tomatoes, bacon and seasoning to taste.

Cook briskly for 10 minutes, stirring all the time.

Spoon the sauce over cooked pasta, sprinkle with grated Parmesan or Pecorino cheese and garnish with a sprig of coriander. Serve immediately.

Serves 4

Variation:

Add 2 tablespoons of wine or vermouth with the tomatoes. Add some fresh chopped red chilli with the pimiento for a slightly stronger flavour.

Three-Cheese Macaroni

Pasta:

250 g (8 oz) wholewheat macaroni

butter

Sauce:

50 g (2 oz) butter or margarine

50 g (2 oz) plain flour

750 ml (1¼ pints) milk

1 teaspoon Worcestershire sauce

chilli powder

½ teaspoon mustard

125 g (4 oz) Gruyère cheese, grated

50 g (2 oz) Mozzarella cheese, grated

3 tablespoons grated Parmesan
  cheese

2 tablespoons fresh white
  breadcrumbs

salt and pepper

sliced pepper, to garnish

Bring a large pan of salted water to the boil.

Add the macaroni to the saucepan, keeping the water boiling. Reduce the heat slightly and cook for 8–10 minutes, or according to the packet instructions, stirring occasionally, until the macaroni is al dente.

Drain the macaroni, rinse with hot water and drain thoroughly in a sieve. Melt a little butter in a saucepan and toss the pasta to coat evenly.

To make the sauce: melt the butter or margarine in a pan, adding the flour to make a roux. When combined, add the milk, Worcestershire sauce, salt and pepper, pinch of chilli powder and mustard. Bring to the boil, stirring.

Reduce the heat and cook gently for 2–3 minutes. Stir in the macaroni until evenly coated in the sauce.

Mix the three cheeses together and reserve one-third for sprinkling. Add the remaining two-thirds to the sauce, mix well and pour into a buttered ovenproof dish.

Sprinkle the top with the remaining cheese and the breadcrumbs.

Place the macaroni cheese under a preheated moderate grill and cook for about 5 minutes until the top is golden brown. Serve immediately garnished with sliced pepper.

Serves 4

left: three-cheese macaroni
right: wholewheat spaghetti with tuna sauce

Spaghetti with Genovese Sauce

250 g (8 oz) spaghetti
salt
basil leaves, to garnish
Sauce:
3 garlic cloves
¼ teaspoon salt
40 g (1½ oz) walnuts
25 g (1 oz) fresh basil leaves, finely
   chopped
50 g (2 oz) grated Parmesan cheese
150 ml (¼ pint) olive oil

Place all the ingredients for the sauce in a blender and blend until smooth. Alternatively, use a pestle and mortar to pound the garlic and salt together, then add the walnuts and then the basil a little at a time, pounding until the mixture is like a purée. Mix in alternate spoonfuls of cheese and oil.

Bring a large pan of salted water to the boil. Coil the pasta into the saucepan, keeping the water boiling. Reduce the heat slightly and cook for 8–10 minutes, or according to the packet instructions, until the pasta is al dente.

Drain the pasta, and pile on to a warmed serving dish, mix in half the sauce, and hand the rest separately. Garnish with basil leaves.

This sauce will keep for up to 2 weeks in a screw-top jar in the refrigerator.

Serves 4

Wholewheat Spaghetti with Tuna Sauce

375 g (12 oz) wholewheat spaghetti
50 g (2 oz) butter
1 garlic clove, finely chopped
2 tablespoons olive oil
200 ml (7 fl oz) chicken stock
3 tablespoons dry sherry
200 g (7 oz) can tuna, drained and
   flaked
3 tablespoons chopped parsley
2 tablespoons single cream
salt and pepper

Bring a large pan of salted water to the boil. Cook the spaghetti for 10–12 minutes, or according to the packet instructions, until al dente. Drain it in a colander and run hot water through it. Drain thoroughly again, return to the pan, stir in half the butter and keep the spaghetti warm.

Fry the garlic in the olive oil and remaining butter over a moderate heat for 2 minutes. Pour on the stock and sherry and boil rapidly for 5 minutes to reduce the liquid. Stir in the tuna fish and 2 tablespoons of the parsley. Add salt and pepper, and stir in the cream. Taste and adjust the seasoning, if necessary.

Turn the spaghetti into a heated serving dish, pour on the sauce and toss lightly to mix. Garnish with the remaining parsley and serve immediately.

Serves 4

Soups and Starters

Chicken Vermicelli Soup

½ tablespoon vegetable oil
2 chicken quarters, skinned
1 onion, chopped
1 carrot, chopped
1 celery stick, chopped
1.5 litres (2½ pints) chicken stock
40 g (1½ oz) vermicelli, broken
    roughly
salt and pepper
1 tablespoon chopped parsley, to
    garnish

Heat the oil in a large saucepan. Add the chicken quarters and brown lightly. Stir in the onion, carrot and celery and cook gently for 5 minutes. Add the stock and some salt and pepper and bring to the boil. Reduce the heat and cover the saucepan with a lid. Cook gently for 1 hour. Remove the chicken from the soup and cut the meat off the bones.

Strain the soup, return it to the saucepan and bring to the boil. Add the vermicelli, keeping the soup boiling, then reduce the heat slightly and cook for 5 minutes.

Stir in the chicken pieces and pour the soup into a warmed tureen or individual bowls. Garnish with chopped parsley.

Serves 4

Mixed Vegetable and Macaroni Soup

25 g (1 oz) butter
1 onion, chopped
1 small leek, trimmed and sliced
1 carrot, diced
1 small turnip, diced
1 celery stick, sliced
¼ small green cabbage, shredded
1.5 litres (2½ pints) vegetable stock or
    water
50 g (2 oz) macaroni
1 tablespoon chopped parsley
salt and pepper
grated Parmesan cheese, to serve

Melt the butter in a large saucepan. Add the onion, leek, carrot, turnip and celery. Cook gently for 5 minutes, stirring occasionally. Stir in the cabbage, stock or water and some salt and pepper to taste, and bring to the boil.
Add the macaroni, keeping the soup boiling, and stir well. Reduce the

heat slightly and cook for
8–10 minutes until the macaroni
is tender.

Serve the soup in a warmed tureen
or individual bowls, sprinkle with
parsley, and offer a separate bowl of
Parmesan cheese.

Serves 4

Sicilian Fish Stew

4 tablespoons olive oil

1 onion, finely sliced

2 celery sticks, sliced

4 garlic cloves, crushed

large pinch of saffron threads or
    1 sachet powdered saffron

375 g (12 oz) ripe tomatoes, skinned
    and roughly chopped

3 tablespoons chopped parsley

2 bay leaves

1.2 litres (2 pints) fish stock or water

150 ml (¼ pint) dry white wine

125 g (4 oz) small pasta shapes, such
    as spirals or bows

1 kg (2 lb) mixed white fish, such as
    monkfish, haddock, cod or mullet,
    skinned, boned and cut into bite-
    sized pieces

salt and pepper

unshelled prawns, to garnish

Heat the oil in a large heavy
saucepan. Add the onion and celery
and stir gently over a low heat until
they have softened. Stir in
the garlic, saffron, tomatoes,

2 tablespoons of the parsley and the
bay leaves and season with salt and
pepper to taste. Cook gently, stirring
to break up the tomatoes, for
5 minutes.

Pour in the stock or water and
the wine and bring to the boil.
Cover and simmer for 15 minutes,
stirring occasionally.

Add the pasta and bring the
liquid back to the boil. Let it boil,
uncovered, for 5 minutes. Reduce
the heat and add the pieces of fish.
Simmer for a further 5 minutes or

until all of the fish and the pasta
are cooked. Taste and adjust the
seasoning if necessary. Serve
garnished with the remaining
parsley and the prawns. Serve with
toasted slices of French bread.

Serves 4–6

*left: mixed vegetable and macaroni
soup*
above: Sicilian fish stew

Country-style Minestrone

This is one of the best known Italian soups, a hearty, warming, peasant dish, substantial enough to provide a whole meal in itself.

125 g (4 oz) cannellini beans
3 tablespoons oil
2 onions, chopped
2 garlic cloves, chopped
2–3 rindless bacon rashers, chopped
1.8 litres (3 pints) water
1 teaspoon chopped marjoram
½ teaspoon chopped thyme
4 tomatoes, skinned, deseeded and chopped
2 carrots, diced
2 potatoes, chopped
1 small turnip, chopped
1–2 celery sticks, chopped
250 g (8 oz) cabbage, shredded
50 g (2 oz) small pasta shapes
3 tablespoons grated Parmesan cheese, plus extra to serve
salt and pepper
To garnish:
1 teaspoon chopped parsley
sprig of thyme

Place the cannellini beans in a large bowl and cover with water. Leave them to soak for 8 hours or overnight. Drain the beans and then rinse them under cold running water.

Heat the oil in a large saucepan and add the onions, garlic and bacon. Sauté gently for about 5 minutes, stirring occasionally, until the onions are soft and golden brown.

Add the beans, water, herbs and tomatoes, cover the pan and simmer gently for 2 hours. Add the carrots and simmer for 10 minutes. Stir in the potatoes and turnip and cook for another 10 minutes.

Add the celery and cabbage to the soup with the pasta shapes and cook for 10 minutes, or until the pasta and all the vegetables are tender. Season to taste with salt and pepper. Stir in the Parmesan and then ladle into individual soup bowls. Serve immediately, sprinkled with extra Parmesan and garnish with parsley and thyme.

Serves 6

Pasta Minestrone

1 tablespoon sunflower oil
1 large onion, chopped
1 garlic clove, chopped
2 carrots, finely sliced
2 celery sticks, finely sliced
1 large potato, diced
1.2 litres (2 pints) beef or chicken stock
375 g (12 oz) tomatoes, peeled and sliced
1 bouquet garni
125 g (4 oz) wholewheat short-cut macaroni
175 g (6 oz) dried flageolet or other beans, boiled until tender and drained
2 courgettes, cut into matchstick strips
3 tablespoons chopped parsley
salt and pepper
grated Parmesan cheese, to serve

Heat the oil in a large pan. Fry the onion and garlic over a moderate heat for 4–5 minutes, stirring once or twice. Add the carrots, celery and potato, pour over the stock and add the tomatoes. Add the bouquet garni and season with salt and pepper.

Bring to the boil, cover the pan and simmer for 30 minutes, stirring occasionally.

Add the macaroni, beans and courgettes, return to the boil, cover and cook for a further 15 minutes.

Taste and adjust the seasoning if necessary. Discard the bouquet garni and stir in the parsley. Serve hot, with the cheese served separately.

Serves 6–8

right: country-style minestrone

Deep-fried Ravioli Pockets

1 x recipe quantity Homemade Egg
   Pasta (see page 8)
oil, for deep-frying
Filling:
125 g (4 oz) full-fat soft cheese
75 g (3 oz) cooked spinach, chopped
2 tablespoons grated Parmesan
   cheese
¼ teaspoon grated nutmeg
Sauce:
1 x recipe quantity Fresh Tomato
   Sauce (see page 14)
4 tablespoons double cream

Make the pasta (see page 8). Wrap in clingfilm and chill for 1 hour.

Meanwhile, make the filling: mix the soft cheese with the spinach, Parmesan cheese and nutmeg. Purée the tomato sauce with the cream in a blender until smooth.

Roll out the pasta dough on a lightly floured surface until very thin. Cut the dough into 2 equal pieces. Spoon 12 portions of filling on to one piece, 5 cm (2 inches) apart. Using a pastry brush, dampen the dough between the mounds of stuffing. Cover the first piece of dough with the second. With the fingertips, press round the dough squares so that the 2 layers stick together. When the layers are stuck, take a pastry wheel, and trim and cut out ravioli squares.

Heat the oil to 180°–190°C (350°–375°F), or until a cube of bread browns in 30 seconds. Deep-fry the ravioli, a few at a time, for about 4–6 minutes until golden and cooked. Drain on kitchen paper and keep warm.

Meanwhile, gently heat the sauce until hot but not boiling. Serve with the ravioli.

Serves 4

White Bean and Vermicelli Soup

250 g (8 oz) dried borlotti or
   cannellini beans, soaked overnight
250 g (8 oz) pork belly with skin
1 onion, chopped
1 carrot, finely chopped
1 celery stick, finely chopped
1 garlic clove, crushed
3 parsley sprigs, finely chopped
1 sprig of sage, chopped
1 bay leaf
175 g (6 oz) vermicelli, spaghetti or
   ribbon noodles
2 tablespoons olive oil
salt and pepper

Drain the beans and put in a large saucepan with the pork, onion, carrot, celery, garlic, parsley, sage, bay leaf and enough water to cover. Bring to the boil, then reduce the heat, cover the pan and simmer gently for 2 hours, or until the beans are soft.

Put one cupful of beans through a food mill or rub through a sieve. Stir the puréed beans back into the soup. Season to taste with salt and pepper and bring back to the boil.

Add the vermicelli, spaghetti or noodles and boil for 8–10 minutes, or according to the packet instructions, until al dente.

Remove the pork from the soup. Cut off the rind and cut the meat into small pieces. Just before serving, drizzle the olive oil on to the soup and stir in the pork. Transfer to a tureen or individual serving dishes.

Serves 4–6

right: prawn and apricot pasta

Prawn and Apricot Pasta

125 g (4 oz) pasta shells
125 g (4 oz) peeled prawns
4 fresh apricots, peeled, stoned and
 sliced
¼ cucumber sliced thinly and halved
salt and pepper
mint sprigs, to garnish

Dressing:
2 tablespoons natural yogurt
2 tablespoons mayonnaise
2 tablespoons grated cucumber
2 teaspoons chopped mint

Cook the pasta in boiling salted water for 10–12 minutes, or according to the packet instructions, until al dente. Drain the pasta, rinse with hot water and drain in a sieve. Allow to cool.

Toss the pasta in a bowl with the prawns, apricots and cucumber.

Mix the yogurt with the mayonnaise, cucumber, mint and salt and pepper to taste. Fold the dressing into the pasta mixture and spoon into 1 large or 4 individual serving dishes. Chill lightly, then serve garnished with mint sprigs

Serves 4

Deep-fried Pasta

This is a traditional pasta recipe from the heart of Italy. These crisp, tasty puffs make excellent nibbles with drinks, and are ideal to serve with savoury sauces and dips.

½ teaspoon dried yeast
¼ teaspoon sugar
500 g (1 lb) plain flour
25 g (1 oz) butter
150 ml (¼ pint) lukewarm chicken stock
vegetable oil, for deep-frying
salt and pepper

Dissolve the yeast and sugar in a little water. Set aside for 10 minutes. Sift the flour and a little salt on to a work surface. Stir in the yeast mixture, then add the butter and enough stock to make a soft dough. Knead well, then roll out to a fairly thick sheet.

Fold the 4 corners of the dough in towards the centre, then flatten with the rolling pin.

Fold and flatten again at least 5 more times. Roll out to a sheet about 5 mm (¼ inch) thick and cut into small rectangles.

Deep-fry the shapes a few at a time in hot oil until golden brown and puffed up. Drain on absorbent kitchen paper while frying the remainder. Sprinkle with salt and pepper, and serve hot.

Serves 6

Spaghetti with Herbed Garlic Oil

250 g (8 oz) plain or wholewheat spaghetti
salt and pepper
sprig of flat leaf parsley, to garnish
4 lemon wedges, to serve
Dressing:
3 tablespoons olive oil
2 garlic cloves, crushed
1 tablespoon chopped basil
1 tablespoon chopped marjoram
1 tablespoon chopped coriander

Cook the spaghetti in plenty of boiling salted water for 8–10 minutes, or according to the packet instructions, until al dente. Drain the spaghetti, rinse with hot water and drain thoroughly.

Place the dressing ingredients in the saucepan. Add the spaghetti and toss well to coat evenly. Place in a warmed serving dish, garnish with parsley or serve individually with a wedge of lemon, accompanied by a mixed green salad, if liked.

Serves 4

left: spaghetti with herbed garlic oil
below: buttered tagliatelle with Parmesan

Buttered Tagliatelle with Parmesan

250 g (8 oz) tagliatelle, plain or verde
40 g (1½ oz) butter
salt and pepper
2 tablespoons grated Parmesan cheese, to serve
1 tablespoon chopped parsley, to garnish

Cook the tagliatelle in plenty of boiling salted water for 5 minutes, or according to the packet instructions, until al dente.

Drain the tagliatelle, rinse with hot water and drain again.

Melt the butter in the saucepan. Add the tagliatelle and toss to coat evenly with the butter.

Transfer the pasta to a warmed serving dish or individual dishes. Sprinkle with some pepper, Parmesan cheese and parsley and serve immediately.

Serves 4

Meat and Poultry

Stuffed Pasta with Tomato Sauce

12 sheets quick-cook egg lasagne

6 slices Parma ham

½ recipe quantity Fresh Tomato Sauce
  (see page 14)

50 g (2 oz) Mozzarella or St Paulin
  cheese, grated

2 tablespoons grated Parmesan
  cheese

sprigs of rosemary, to garnish

Filling:

25 g (1 oz) butter or margarine

250 g (8 oz) button mushrooms,
  finely chopped

½ teaspoon chopped rosemary

2 tablespoons plain flour

2 tablespoons lemon juice

4 tablespoons single cream

salt and pepper

Cook the lasagne in plenty of boiling salted water, feed in a few sheets at a time, keeping the water boiling. Reduce the heat and cook for 2–3 minutes or according to packet instructions. Remove the lasagne and place, sheets separated, on a board. Repeat to cook the remaining lasagne. Place half a slice of ham on each sheet of lasagne.

To make the filling: melt the butter or margarine in a small saucepan, add the mushrooms and rosemary and fry quickly for 1 minute. Stir in the flour and cook for 1 minute, then stir in the lemon juice. Remove the pan from the heat. Stir in the cream and some pepper and divide the filling between the sheets of lasagne. Spread the filling evenly over the ham and roll up firmly.

Pour half the tomato sauce into a greased, shallow ovenproof dish. Arrange the lasagne rolls in the dish and pour over the remaining sauce. Sprinkle with Mozzarella or St Paulin and Parmesan and cover with a piece of buttered foil. Cook in the centre of a preheated oven, 190°C (375°F), Gas Mark 5, for 25–30 minutes until the pasta is tender. Remove the foil after 20 minutes of the cooking time.

Serve hot, garnished with sprigs of rosemary and accompanied by green beans, if liked.

Serves 4

Variation:

For an alternative filling, you can use chopped, cooked spinach and cream or cottage cheese.

Beef and Noodle Casserole

175 g (6 oz) tagliatelle verde
750 g (1½ lb) minced beef
2 onions, chopped
1–2 garlic cloves, crushed
2 teaspoons cornflour
425 g (14 oz) can tomatoes
150 g (¼ pint) beef stock
1 tablespoon soy sauce
1 tablespoon Worcestershire sauce
1 tablespoon tomato purée
1 teaspoon dried oregano
25 g (1 oz) butter
25 g (1 oz) plain flour
300 ml (½ pint) milk
40–50 g (1½–2 oz) mature Cheddar
  cheese, grated
salt and pepper
bay leaves, to garnish

Cook the tagliatelle in plenty of boiling salted water for 5 minutes until partly cooked. Drain, rinse in hot water and drain again in a sieve.

Cook the minced beef gently in a pan with no extra fat until browned and crumbly, stirring frequently. Add the onions and garlic, and continue cooking for 3–4 minutes. Blend the cornflour with some of the juice from the tomatoes, then stir into the beef with the tomatoes, stock, soy sauce, Worcestershire sauce, tomato purée, oregano, and salt and pepper to taste. Bring to the boil and cook for 2 minutes.

Place half the tagliatelle in the base of a casserole, cover with the meat mixture, then add the remaining pasta. Melt the butter in a pan, stir in the flour and cook for 1 minute, gradually add the milk and bring to the boil for 1 minute. Season with salt and pepper to taste and pour over the noodles. Sprinkle over the cheese.

Cover and cook in a preheated oven, 200° (400°F), Gas Mark 6, for 15 minutes, then uncover and continue cooking for a further 10–15 minutes or until the topping is brown and crispy. Serve hot, garnished with bay leaves.

Serves 4–5

Rigatoni with Cheese and Sausage

250 g (8 oz) Italian sausage, skinned and chopped
500 ml (17 fl oz) water
250 g (8 oz) ricotta cheese
425 g (14 oz) rigatoni
75 g (3 oz) Pecorino cheese, grated
salt and pepper

Put the sausage and water into a pan, cover and boil until the sausage is tender and the fat rises to the surface. Skim off the fat and reserve. Drain the sausage.

Put the ricotta cheese in a bowl and beat well to soften. Add the fat from the sausage and season with salt and pepper to taste.

Cook the rigatoni in plenty of boiling salted water for 10–12 minutes, or according to the packet instructions, until al dente. Drain the rigatoni, rinse with hot water and drain thoroughly.

Add the rigatoni, sausage and Pecorino to the ricotta mixture and fold gently to mix. Serve immediately.

Serves 4

---

below: rigatoni with cheese and sausage
right: tagliatelle with borlotti beans and sage

Rabbit with Baked Garlic and Chocolate Noodles

3 tablespoons plain flour
1 x 1.25–1.5 kg (2½–3 lb) rabbit, cut into serving pieces
3–4 tablespoons olive oil
1 large onion, chopped
250 ml (8 fl oz) dry white wine
150 ml (¼ pint) fresh orange juice
300 ml (½ pint) chicken stock
50 g (2 oz) roasted ground hazelnuts
2 sprigs of thyme
1 bay leaf
4 small whole heads of garlic
salt and pepper
Chocolate noodles:
275 g (9 oz) pasta flour
25 g (1 oz) cocoa powder
pinch of salt
1 tablespoon olive oil
3–4 eggs, beaten

Season the flour with salt and pepper and toss the rabbit pieces in the flour, shaking off any excess. Heat 2 tablespoons of the oil in a large flameproof casserole, add the rabbit pieces and brown well all over. Transfer to a plate.

Add the onion to the casserole, adding more oil if necessary, and cook for 6–8 minutes until softened. Add the wine and orange juice, bring to the boil and boil rapidly for 3 minutes or until reduced by half.

Add the remaining ingredients, except for the garlic.

Return the rabbit pieces to the casserole and bring back to the boil. Season with salt and pepper and place the heads of garlic on top. Reduce the heat, cover with a tight-fitting lid and place in a preheated oven, 160°C (325°F), Gas Mark 3, for 1–1½ hours until tender.

To make the chocolate noodles: sift the flour, cocoa and salt into the bowl of a food processor. Add the oil and 3 of the eggs and process until the dough starts to come together. (If it looks dry, add a little more beaten egg.) Alternatively make the dough by hand. Turn out on a lightly floured surface and knead for 5 minutes until smooth. Wrap in clingfilm and leave to rest in the refrigerator for 30 minutes.

Divide the dough into 3 pieces and roll out each piece on a clean surface, rotating the dough occasionally, until it is very thin. Lift on to a clean dry towel and leave to dry for 5–10 minutes.

Return each piece of dough to the work surface and roll up loosely lengthways. Cut across into 1 cm (½ inch) strips, then carefully unroll the noodles, or use a pasta machine to roll and cut the pasta.

Bring a large pan of salted water to the boil. Add the noodles, stirring once to make sure they do not stick and cook for 2–4 minutes or until al dente. Drain the noodles and serve with the rabbit.

Serves 4

Tagliatelle with Borlotti Beans and Sage

3 tablespoons olive oil
75 g (3 oz) smoked bacon, derinded and cubed
1 onion, chopped
5 sage leaves
200 g (7 oz) can borlotti beans
2 tablespoons hot chicken stock
¼ teaspoon flour
1 tablespoon tomato purée
2 tablespoons red wine
425 g (14 oz) tagliatelle
2 tablespoons grated Parmesan cheese
1 tablespoon grated Pecorino cheese
sage leaves, to garnish

Heat the oil in a large, heavy-based pan, add the bacon, onion and whole sage leaves. Cook over a medium heat until golden.

Drain the canned borlotti beans, rinse and drain again, then add to the pan.

Heat the stock. Mix the flour and tomato purée in a small bowl; stir in the hot stock and the wine.

Pour into the bean mixture, stir with a wooden spoon and simmer over a low heat until the sauce thickens.

Cook the tagliatelle in plenty of boiling salted water for 5 minutes, or according to the packet instructions, until al dente.

Remove the sage leaves from the sauce, taste and adjust the seasoning if necessary. Drain the pasta, mix with the sauce and put in a large heated serving dish. Add the Parmesan and Pecorino, and serve hot, garnished with a few sage leaves.

Serves 4

Baked Rigatoni

1 thick slice day-old bread
150 g (5 oz) minced beef
75 g (3 oz) Pecorino cheese, grated
1 egg, beaten
1 tablespoon chopped parsley
1 garlic clove, crushed
4 tablespoons olive oil
150 g (5 oz) Italian sausage, diced
200 ml (7 fl oz) red wine
425 g (14 oz) tomatoes, peeled and
    chopped
300 g (10 oz) rigatoni
3 hard-boiled eggs, sliced
125 g (4 oz) Provola cheese, sliced
salt and pepper

Soak the bread in lukewarm water, then squeeze dry. Combine the beef, one-third of the Pecorino, the egg, parsley, garlic and salt and pepper to taste. Stir well to mix, then shape into small balls, about the size of walnuts.

Heat the oil in a pan, add the sausage and meatballs and cook over a moderate heat for 10 minutes. Add the wine and simmer until it has evaporated, then add the tomatoes and salt and pepper to taste. Lower the heat and simmer for 40 minutes.

Meanwhile, cook the rigatoni in plenty of boiling salted water for 10–12 minutes, or according to the packet instructions, until al dente. Drain the rigatoni, rinse with hot water and drain thoroughly.

Line the bottom of a buttered deep ovenproof dish with a layer of the sauce, cover with a layer of rigatoni, then sprinkle with Pecorino. Cover with a layer of sliced egg, then a layer of Provola. Continue with these layers until all the ingredients are used, finishing with a layer of sauce and a sprinkling of Pecorino. Bake in a preheated oven, 200°C (400°F), Gas Mark 6, for 15 minutes. Serve hot.

Serves 4

Chicken and Herb Pasta

125 g (4 oz) pasta shells
1 teaspoon chopped oregano
1 teaspoon chopped rosemary
375 g (12 oz) cooked chicken
125 g (4 oz) mushrooms, chopped
1 tablespoon olive oil
1 teaspoon ground coriander
salt and pepper

Cook the pasta in boiling salted water with the herbs for about 5 minutes.

Cut the chicken meat into bite-sized pieces. Add the chicken and mushrooms to the pasta and cook for a further 8–10 minutes. Drain if necessary. Add the olive oil and coriander. Season with salt and pepper just before serving. This dish can also be served cold.

Serves 4

Penne with Chilli Sauce

1–2 tablespoons olive oil
1 large onion, finely chopped
2 garlic cloves, crushed
125 g (4 oz) rindless streaky bacon,
    chopped
1–2 fresh red chillies, chopped
425 g (14 oz) can chopped tomatoes
75 g (3 oz) Pecorino or Parmesan
    cheese, shaved
500 g (1 lb) penne
salt and pepper

Heat the oil in a pan and cook the onion, garlic and bacon until they are lightly coloured.

Add the chillies, tomatoes and 25 g (1 oz) of the cheese. Season with salt and pepper to taste. Cook over a gentle heat for 30–40 minutes until the sauce thickens. Check and adjust the seasoning.

Cook the penne in boiling salted water for 10–12 minutes, or according to the packet instructions, until al dente. Drain well and place in a hot serving dish.

Stir in most of the sauce, mix well and then pour the remaining sauce over the top. Garnish with shavings of Pecorino or Parmesan and serve the remaining cheese separately.

Serves 4

right: penne with chilli sauce

Pork and Sweet Peppers with Tagliatelle

50 g (2 oz) butter
1 tablespoon vegetable oil
500 g (1 lb) pork fillet, cut into strips
1 large Spanish onion, finely sliced
425 g (14 oz) can sweet peppers, drained and cut into squares
1 teaspoon coriander seeds
pinch of caster sugar
150 ml (¼ pint) white or rosé wine
250 g (8 oz) tagliatelle
150 ml (5 fl oz) soured cream
paprika, to sprinkle
salt and pepper
sprig of sage, to garnish

Heat the butter and oil in a large heavy-based pan and, when sizzling, add the pork strips a few at a time. Fry over a moderate heat for 2–3 minutes, turning frequently, to seal and brown on all sides. Using a slotted spoon, transfer the pork to a casserole and fry the remaining pork in batches in the same way. Lower the heat, add the onion to the pan and fry over a gentle heat for about 10 minutes, until soft and light golden. Add the peppers, stir well to mix, then add the coriander and sugar, and season with salt and pepper to taste.

Pour the wine into the pan, bring to the boil and allow to bubble over a moderate heat for 1–2 minutes, stirring and scraping the sides and base of the pan to remove any sediment. Pour into the casserole, cover and cook in a preheated oven, 190°C (375°F), Gas Mark 5, for 1 hour, until the pork is tender.

Meanwhile, cook the tagliatelle in boiling salted water for 5 minutes, or according to the packet instructions, until al dente. Drain, rinse with hot water and drain.

Using the slotted spoon, transfer the pork and vegetables to a warmed serving dish and keep warm. Stir the soured cream into the sauce in the casserole. Reheat gently on the hob without boiling and pour over the pork and vegetables. Sprinkle with paprika. garnish with sage and serve with the tagliatelle.

Serves 4

Liver Stroganoff

25 g (1 oz) butter
1 onion, chopped
500 g (1 lb) lamb's liver, sliced into very thin strips
1 tablespoon tomato purée
1 tablespoon Worcestershire sauce
juice of 1 lemon
250 g (8 oz) button mushrooms, sliced
250 g (8 oz) pasta twists
a little olive oil (optional)
150 ml (¼ pint) soured cream
salt and pepper

Melt the butter in a pan, add the onion and fry over gentle heat until soft. Add the liver and fry for 5 minutes, stirring constantly.

Stir in the remaining ingredients except for the pasta, oil and soured cream, then cook for a further 5 minutes, stirring occasionally.

Meanwhile, cook the pasta twists in boiling salted water for 10–12 minutes, or according to the packet instructions, until al dente. Drain, add a few drops of oil, if liked, and keep warm.

Remove the liver pan from the heat, stir in the cream, then return to a low heat and warm through without boiling. Adjust the seasoning and serve with the pasta.

Serves 4

left: pork and sweet peppers with tagliatelle
right: spiced lamb with pasta

Spiced Lamb with Pasta

50 g (2 oz) butter
1 onion, finely chopped
1 garlic clove, crushed
½ teaspoon ground cinnamon
625 g (1¼ lb) lamb fillet, cut into thin slices
2 teaspoons cornflour
150 ml (¼ pint) chicken stock
150 ml (¼ pint) soured cream
1 tablespoon chopped mint
250 g (8 oz) tagliatelle
salt and pepper
chopped mint, plus a sprig, to garnish

Melt the butter in a frying pan. Add the onion, garlic and cinnamon and fry gently until the onion softens. Add the slices of lamb fillet and cook steadily, turning occasionally, until the lamb is coloured on all sides.

Blend the cornflour with the stock and soured cream and add to the pan. Stir until the sauce thickens slightly. Add the mint, season with salt and pepper to taste, and simmer gently for 8–10 minutes until tender.

Meanwhile, cook the tagliatelle in boiling salted water for 5 minutes, or according to the packet instructions, until al dente. Drain the tagliatelle, rinse with hot water and drain thoroughly in a sieve.

Divide the tagliatelle between 4 warmed plates. Top with the lamb and garnish with the mint.

Serves 4

Layered Pasta with a Parmesan and Meat Sauce

1 x quantity Bolognese Sauce (see page 14)
250 g (8 oz) quick-cook dried lasagne sheets, or freshly made lasagne
50 g (2 oz) grated Parmesan cheese
15 g (½ oz) butter

Béchamel sauce:
40 g (1½ oz) butter
40 g (1½ oz) flour
600 ml (1 pint) milk
pinch of ground nutmeg
salt and pepper

Make the bolognese sauce, and simmer gently for at least 1 hour until it is time to assemble the lasagne.

Make the béchamel sauce: melt the butter in a saucepan and stir in the flour. Cook over a gentle heat, without browning, for 2–3 minutes and then gradually beat in the milk until you have a thick, smooth glossy sauce. Season with nutmeg, salt and pepper, and cook gently for 5–10 minutes.

Put a little of the bolognese sauce in a buttered ovenproof dish and cover with a layer of lasagne and then another layer of bolognese sauce, topped with some béchamel sauce. Continue layering up in this way, ending with a layer of lasagne and a topping of béchamel.

Sprinkle with grated Parmesan and then dot the top with butter. Bake in a preheated oven, 230°C (450°F), Gas Mark 8, for 30 minutes until the lasagne is golden brown.

Serves 4

Baked Meat Lasagne

4 tablespoons olive oil
2 onions, chopped
3 garlic cloves, crushed
2 celery sticks, chopped
500 g (1 lb) minced beef
125 g (4 oz) chicken livers, chopped
400 ml (14 fl oz) dry white wine
2 x 425 g (14 oz) cans tomatoes
½ teaspoon grated nutmeg
1 teaspoon dried mixed herbs
8 sheets quick-cook lasagne verdi
300 ml (½ pint) Béchamel sauce (see above page left)

50 g (2 oz) Parmesan cheese, grated
25 g (1 oz) matured Cheddar cheese, grated
1 tablespoon dried breadcrumbs
salt and pepper

Heat the oil in a large pan, add the onions and 2 garlic cloves and cook for 10 minutes, until pale golden. Stir in the celery and cook for 2 minutes.

Increase the heat and add the minced beef. Cook rapidly until lightly browned. Add the chicken livers, and season liberally with salt and pepper.

Pour over the wine, add the tomatoes with their juice, nutmeg and herbs. Bring to the boil, cover and simmer very gently for 2½–3 hours, stirring occasionally; if the mixture becomes too thick, add a little more wine. Stir in the remaining garlic and check the seasoning.

Spoon enough sauce into a large ovenproof dish or roasting tin to cover the base. Arrange some lasagne over this. Repeat the layers until all the sauce and lasagne are used, finishing with lasagne.

Spoon over the Béchamel sauce and sprinkle with the cheeses and breadcrumbs.

Bake in a preheated oven, 200°C (400°F), Gas Mark 6, for 45–50 minutes, until golden. Serve immediately.

Serves 6–8

Turkey Breasts in Cider Cream Sauce

2 tablespoon oil
2 small onions, sliced
2 x 250 g (8 oz) turkey breasts
2 tablespoons plain flour
400 ml (14 fl oz) dry cider
3 large red peppers, deseeded and sliced
250 g (8 oz) tagliatelle
1 tablespoon single cream
salt and pepper

Heat the oil in a frying pan. Add the onions and fry until soft but not brown. Cut the turkey breasts into 8 pieces and coat in the flour. Add to the pan and brown on all sides. Remove the turkey from the pan. Stir in any remaining flour and cook for 1 minute. Add the cider gradually, stirring constantly. Season to taste and bring to the boil. Return the turkey to the pan with the red pepper. Reduce the heat and cook gently for 15–20 minutes, until the turkey is cooked.

Meanwhile, cook the tagliatelle in boiling salted water for 5 minutes, or according to packet instructions, until al dente. Drain thoroughly.

Place the tagliatelle in a warmed serving dish. Remove the turkey mixture from the heat and stir in the cream. Pour over the tagliatelle and serve immediately.

Serves 4

left: layered pasta with a Parmesan and meat sauce
above: *turkey breasts in cider cream sauce*

Turkey Milanese

375 g (12 oz) cooked turkey meat

125 g (4 oz) pasta twists

250 g (8 oz) canned artichoke hearts, drained

2 teaspoons oregano, chopped

salt and pepper

Cut the turkey into bite-sized pieces.

Cook the pasta in plenty of boiling salted water for 10–12 minutes, or according to the packet instructions, until al dente. Drain and return to the saucepan.

Add the turkey, drained artichoke hearts and oregano to the pan and place over a gentle heat, stirring, until thoroughly heated through. Taste and adjust the seasoning. Pour into a warmed dish and serve.

Serves 4

Sausages with Tagliatelle

4 large herb-flavoured pork sausages

4 thick bacon rashers, derinded

25 g (1 oz) butter

2 tablespoons vegetable oil

1 onion, chopped

1½ teaspoons dried sage

1½ tablespoons plain flour

150 ml (¼ pint) chicken stock

150 ml (¼ pint) soured cream

250 g (8 oz) tagliatelle

salt and pepper

chopped parsley, to garnish

Wrap each sausage in a bacon rasher and secure with fine string.

Heat the butter and oil in a flameproof casserole, add the onion and fry gently for 5 minutes until softened but not brown. Add the sausages and the onion and sage and fry for a further 5 minutes, turning occasionally, until the bacon is browned. Set aside the sausages and remove the string.

Sprinkle the flour into the casserole and cook, stirring, for 1 minute. Stir in the stock gradually. Bring to the boil, then season to taste with salt and pepper and stir in the soured cream. Return the sausages to the casserole, cover and simmer for 20 minutes until tender.

Meanwhile, cook the tagliatelle in plenty of boiling salted water for 5 minutes, or according to the packet instructions, until al dente. Drain the tagliatelle, rinse with hot water and drain thoroughly. Pile the sausages on top of the pasta, garnish with parsley and serve.

Serves 4

left: sausages with tagliatelle
right: wild rabbit braised with red wine and olives

Wild Rabbit Braised with Red Wine and Olives

7 tablespoons olive oil

1.25 kg (2½ lb) wild rabbit, cut into serving pieces

2 garlic cloves, chopped

1 rosemary sprig, chopped

200 ml (7 fl oz) red wine

6–8 tablespoons chicken stock

2 tomatoes, skinned and mashed

250 g (8 oz) black olives, halved and pitted

250 g (8 oz) tagliatelle

salt and pepper

Heat the oil in a flameproof casserole, add the rabbit and sprinkle with the garlic and rosemary.

Fry gently until the rabbit is browned on all sides, turning frequently.

Add the wine and salt and pepper to taste. Cover and simmer for 30 minutes, adding a little stock to moisten as necessary.

Add the tomatoes and olives and cook for a further 40 minutes until the rabbit is tender. Cook the pasta in plenty of boiling salted water for 5 minutes, or according to the packet instructions, until al dente. Drain well and transfer to a heated serving bowl. Spoon the rabbit sauce over the tagliatelle and serve.

Serves 4

Paprika Pork with Caraway Noodles

1–2 tablespoons olive oil

75 g (3 oz) rindless streaky bacon, chopped

2 onions, chopped

2 garlic cloves, crushed

2 teaspoons paprika

250 g (8 oz) tomatoes, skinned and chopped

1 tablespoon tomato purée

1.25 kg (2½ lb) boneless shoulder of pork, trimmed and cut into 3.5 cm (1½ inch) cubes

50 g (2 oz) small pickled gherkins, cut into strips

1 tablespoon plain flour

75 ml (3 fl oz) soured cream

salt and pepper

chopped parsley, to garnish

Caraway noodles:

200 g (7 oz) plain flour

½ teaspoon salt

2 teaspoons caraway seeds, crushed

1 egg, lightly beaten

1 tablespoon vegetable oil

4 tablespoons water

Heat 1 tablespoon of the oil in a large flameproof casserole over a moderate heat, add the bacon and cook for 1–2 minutes until it renders some fat. Reduce the heat and add the onions and garlic, adding more oil if necessary, and cook for 5–6 minutes until softened. Add the paprika and cook for 1–2 minutes.

Add the tomatoes, tomato purée and the pork to the pan, with about 600 ml (1 pint) water to cover. Season with salt and pepper and stir well. Bring to the boil, reduce the heat, cover and simmer gently for

1–1½ hours until the meat is tender.

To make the noodles, sift the flour into a food processor, add the remaining ingredients and process to form a soft dough. Alternatively mix together by hand. Knead the dough on a lightly floured surface for 5 minutes. Wrap in clingfilm and chill for 30 minutes.

Divide the dough into 3 and roll out each piece on a clean work surface, rotating the dough occasionally, until it is very thin. Lift the dough on to a clean dry towel and leave to dry for about 5–10 minutes.

Return each piece of dough to the work surface and roll up loosely lengthways. Cut across into thin strips and then carefully unroll the noodles. Alternatively use a pasta machine to roll and cut the pasta.

When the meat is tender, stir the pickled gherkins into the casserole. In a small bowl mix the flour with the soured cream to form a smooth paste. Stir thoroughly into the sauce and continue cooking for 10 minutes.

Drop the noodles into a large saucepan of gently boiling salted water and cook for 2–4 minutes or until al dente. Drain well and serve with the stew, sprinkled with chopped parsley.

Serves 4

---

left: paprika pork with caraway noodles

Chicken and Macaroni Pie

200 g (7 oz) dried short-cut macaroni

1 tablespoon olive oil

2 onions, finely chopped

200 g (7 oz) boneless chicken breast, skinned and cut into 5 mm (¼ inch) dice

200 g (7 oz) button mushrooms, quartered

3 tablespoons chopped parsley

25 g (1 oz) butter

25 g (1 oz) plain flour

450 ml (¾ pint) milk

125 g (4 oz) Mozzarella cheese, grated

pinch of chilli powder

2 eggs, beaten

butter, for greasing

6 tablespoons dried wholemeal breadcrumbs

salt and pepper

Bring a large pan of salted water to the boil, add the macaroni stir and bring back to the boil. Reduce the heat and boil, uncovered, for 8–10 minutes, or according to the packet instructions, until al dente. Drain it thoroughly.

Heat the oil in a heavy saucepan. Add the onions and cook over a moderate heat, stirring frequently, for about 5 minutes until they are golden. Add the diced chicken and stir-fry for 5 minutes. Add the mushrooms and continue cooking for a further 5 minutes. Remove from the heat. Stir in the parsley and season with salt and pepper to taste.

Melt the butter in a small heavy saucepan. Add the flour and cook, stirring, for 1 minute. Gradually blend in the milk and bring to the boil, still stirring. Simmer for 3 minutes. Add the Mozzarella, chilli powder and salt and pepper to taste. Stir the sauce until the cheese has melted. Remove the pan from the heat and leave the sauce to cool slightly. Stir in first the beaten eggs and then the macaroni.

Brush the inside of a 20 cm (8 inch) spring-form cake tin liberally with butter. Coat it evenly with 4 tablespoons of the breadcrumbs.

Pour half the macaroni mixture into the tin and level the surface. Spoon the chicken mixture on top and cover with the remaining breadcrumbs.

Bake the pie in a preheated oven, 190°C, (375°F), Gas Mark 5, for 35 minutes, or until it feels set in the centre when pressed. Remove from the oven and allow to stand for 10 minutes. Loosen the side of the tin and slide the 'pie' on to a warm serving plate. Serve hot with a tomato salad, if liked.

Serves 4–6

Italian Beef Bake

350 g (12 oz) minced beef
4 rashers streaky bacon, derinded and
  chopped
1 onion, chopped
1 celery stick, finely chopped
50 g (2 oz) button mushrooms, finely
  chopped
1 garlic clove, crushed
½ tablespoon plain flour
250 g (8 oz) can tomatoes
1 tablespoon tomato purée
¼ teaspoon dried marjoram
150 ml (¼ pint) beef or chicken stock
pinch of grated nutmeg (optional)
250 g (8 oz) spaghetti
75 g (3 oz) Mozzarella cheese, grated
15 g (½ oz) Parmesan cheese, grated
3 tomatoes, sliced
salt and pepper

Put the beef and bacon in a
non-stick saucepan and fry for
5 minutes, stirring well. Add the
onion, celery, mushrooms and
garlic and fry over a moderate heat
for 3 minutes, stirring often.

Add the flour and cook for
1 minute, then add the tomatoes
with their juice, breaking them up
coarsely with a wooden spoon. Stir
in the tomato purée, marjoram,
stock, salt and pepper to taste and
the nutmeg, if using. Bring to the
boil, then lower the heat and
simmer, uncovered, for 15 minutes.

Meanwhile, cook the spaghetti in
a large saucepan of boiling salted
water for 8–10 minutes, or
according to the packet
instructions, until al dente. Drain
well, then rinse with boiling water.

Place the drained, cooked
spaghetti in a greased, shallow
ovenproof dish, spoon over the meat
sauce and sprinkle with the cheeses.
Arrange the tomatoes on top.

Bake in a preheated oven, 190°C
(375°F), Gas Mark 5, for 25–30
minutes until golden brown. Serve
hot with a green salad, if liked.

Serves 4–5

Pasta with Prosciutto and Pea Sauce

50 g (2 oz) butter
250 g (8 oz) prosciutto, diced
300 g (10 oz) frozen petit pois,
  defrosted
6 spring onions, green parts included,
  finely sliced
300 ml (½ pint) whipping cream
50 g (2 oz) Parmesan cheese, grated
500 g (1 lb) pasta shells
salt and pepper

Melt the butter in a pan, add the
prosciutto, and gently fry for
1–2 minutes until lightly browned.
Add the peas and spring onions,
and fry for 2–3 minutes.

Pour in the cream, and season
lightly with salt and pepper. Simmer
over a medium-high heat, stirring
constantly, until thickened. Stir in
the Parmesan cheese.

Cook the pasta in boiling salted
water for 10–12 minutes, or
according to the packet
instructions, until al dente. Drain
the pasta well and toss with the
sauce. Serve immediately.

Serves 4–6

Ravioli with Chicken

125 g (4 oz) butter
1 small onion, chopped
50 g (2 oz) button mushrooms, diced
750 g (1½ lb) cooked chicken, minced
125 ml (4 fl oz) dry white wine
125 ml (4 fl oz) single cream
1 tablespoon chopped parsley
1 recipe quantity Homemade Egg
  Pasta (see page 8)
1 egg, beaten
4–6 tablespoons grated Parmesan
  cheese
salt and pepper
parsley sprigs, to garnish

Melt 25 g (1 oz) of the butter in a
pan, add the onion and cook for
5 minutes, without browning. Add
the mushrooms and cook for
2 minutes.

Remove from the heat and stir in
the chicken, wine, cream, parsley,
and salt and pepper to taste. Leave
until cold.

Cut the pasta dough in half.
Cover with clingfilm and rest for
30 minutes. Roll out the pasta
dough thinly.

Place teaspoons of the chicken
mixture about 5 cm (2 inches) apart
on one piece of pasta. Brush lightly
with beaten egg between the filling.

Lay the second sheet of pasta
lightly on top, pressing down
between the filling to seal. Cut
around the filling with a pastry
wheel or knife to give little ravioli
squares. Check that each ravioli is
thoroughly sealed and place on a
board to dry for 1 hour.

Cook for 4–5 minutes or until al
dente. Transfer to a warmed serving
dish with a slotted spoon. Add the
remaining butter and toss well.
Sprinkle with Parmesan to taste,
garnish with parsley and serve.

Serves 6

---

left: Italian beef bake
above: pasta with prosciutto and pea sauce

Pasta with Chicken Livers

1 tablespoon oil

50 g (2 oz) butter

4 shallots, chopped

4 rashers back bacon, derinded and chopped

250 g (8 oz) minced beef

150 ml (¼ pint) each dry Vermouth and dry white wine

375 g (12 oz) tomatoes, skinned, deseeded and chopped

2 cloves garlic, crushed

2 tablespoons each chopped parsley, marjoram and sage

250 g (8 oz) chicken livers, chopped

500 g (1 lb) dried pasta twists

salt and pepper

Heat the oil and half the butter in a pan, add the shallots and cook, stirring constantly, for 2–3 minutes without browning. Add the bacon and minced beef, increase the heat and brown quickly, stirring.

Add the Vermouth and wine and boil rapidly for 15 minutes. Stir in the tomatoes and season. Stir in the garlic and herbs. Add the chicken livers and cook for 3 minutes.

Cook the pasta for 10–12 minutes, or according to the packet instructions, until al dente. Drain thoroughly, turn into a warmed serving dish, add the remaining butter and toss well. Spoon the sauce over the pasta, toss and serve.

Serves 6

Shells with Pâté and Cream

300 g (10 oz) pasta shells or twists

75 g (3 oz) fine, smooth liver pâté, at room temperature

1–2 teaspoons garlic purée, to taste

4 tablespoons dry white wine (optional)

150 ml (¼ pint) single cream

300 g (10 oz) can whole button mushrooms, drained

salt and pepper

sprigs of tarragon, to garnish

Bring a saucepan of salted water to the boil. Add the pasta shells, stir reduce the heat and boil, uncovered, for 10–12 minutes, or according to the packet instructions, stirring occasionally, until al dente.

Meanwhile, put the pâté in a heavy saucepan with the garlic purée and the wine, if using, or 4 tablespoons of the pasta cooking water. Beat them together well. Gradually beat in all but 4 tablespoons of the cream until it is evenly incorporated. Stir in the mushrooms. Place the saucepan over a gentle heat, stir until the sauce is heated through and season.

Drain the pasta well and divide equally between 4 warm soup plates. Pour over the sauce. Garnish with tarragon sprigs. Serve this dish at once with chilled dry white wine.

Serves 4

Pasta with Ham and Vegetables

250 g (8 oz) wholewheat pasta shapes

375 g (12 oz) aubergines, diced

1 tablespoon salt

4 tablespoons olive or sunflower oil

1 large onion, finely sliced

1 garlic clove, finely chopped

2 red peppers, deseeded and cut into strips

2 green peppers, deseeded and cut into strips

375 g (12 oz) tomatoes, skinned and chopped

375 g (12 oz) lean ham, diced

Cook the pasta shapes in plenty of boiling salted water for 12–14 minutes, or according to the packet instructions, until al dente. Drain, rinse in hot water and drain again.

Place the aubergines in a colander and sprinkle with the salt. Leave for 20 minutes. Rinse under cold water and dry with kitchen paper.

Heat the oil in a saucepan on a low heat. Add the onion and garlic, and cook for 2 minutes. Mix in the aubergines and peppers. Cover and cook for 10 minutes. Add the tomatoes and ham. Cover and cook for a further 10 minutes. Mix in the pasta and reheat before serving.

Serves 4

---

right: shells with pâté and cream

Pasta Pot

200 g (7 oz) can tomatoes

1 tablespoon, plus 1 teaspoon
   vegetable oil

½ small onion, finely chopped

2 teaspoons tomato purée

½ teaspoon caster sugar

150 ml (¼ pint) vegetable stock or
   water

125 g (4 oz) macaroni or other small
   pasta shapes

300 ml (½ pint) milk

25 g (1 oz) plain flour

25 g (1 oz) butter

1 egg, beaten

2–3 salami sticks, chopped into bite-
   sized pieces

salt and pepper

Put the tomatoes in a blender or food processor with the 1 tablespoon oil, the onion, tomato purée and sugar. Process to a purée, then turn into a saucepan. Add the stock or water and salt and pepper to taste, and simmer for 15 minutes, stirring occasionally.

Meanwhile, cook the macaroni in plenty of boiling salted water, to which the remaining 1 teaspoon oil has been added, for 8–10 minutes, or according to the packet instructions, until al dente. Drain, rinse with hot water and drain thoroughly in a sieve.

Put the milk, flour and butter in the blender or food processor and process for 1 minute to combine. Turn into a saucepan and bring to the boil, then simmer for 5 minutes, stirring until thickened. Remove from the heat, leave to cool for 12 minutes, then beat in the egg with salt and pepper to taste.

Fold the chopped salami into the tomato sauce, then fold in the pasta. Turn into an ovenproof dish and pour the white sauce over the top. Cook in a preheated oven, 180°C (350°F), Gas Mark 4, for 15–20 minutes until bubbling. Serve hot. A mixed green salad makes a good accompaniment.

Serves 2–3

Penne with a Spicy Sausage Sauce

3 tablespoons oil
25 g (1 oz) butter
½ onion, chopped
½ small shallot, chopped
1 small carrot, finely sliced
1 celery stick, sliced
125 g (4 oz) salamelle sausage, crumbled
½ small yellow sweet pepper, deseeded and diced
4 basil leaves, torn
50 ml (2 fl oz) dry red wine
425 g (14 oz) penne
2 tablespoons grated Pecorino cheese
2 tablespoons grated Parmesan cheese
few basil leaves, to garnish

Heat the oil and butter in a flameproof casserole, add the onion, shallot, carrot and celery, and cook over a low heat for 4 minutes.

Mix well, then add the crumbled sausage, diced pepper and torn basil leaves. Brown over a medium heat for 3–4 minutes, and moisten with red wine.

Cook the penne in lightly salted boiling water for 10–12 minutes, or according to the packet instructions, until al dente.

Transfer the penne to a heated serving dish and pour on the sausage and vegetable sauce.

Sprinkle with the cheeses and mix well before serving, garnished with the basil leaves.

Serves 4

Fish and Shellfish

Spaghetti with Mussel and Tomato Sauce

1 kg (2 lb) fresh mussels

3 tablespoons olive oil

1 onion, chopped

1 garlic clove, crushed

500 g (1 lb) tomatoes, skinned and chopped, or 425 g (14 oz) can chopped tomatoes

2 teaspoons tomato purée

3 tablespoons dry white wine

375 g (12 oz) spaghetti

salt and pepper

1 tablespoon chopped parsley, to garnish

Discard any opened mussels. Scrub the remainder, remove the beards and wash them thoroughly in cold water. Place them in a large pan, cover and cook over a high heat for 4 minutes, stirring once or twice.

Lift out the mussels, discarding any unopened ones, and remove the others from their shells.

Drain the liquid into a small pan through a sieve lined with muslin and boil to reduce to 2 tablespoons.

Heat the oil in a pan and fry the onion and garlic for 4–5 minutes. Add the tomatoes, tomato purée, mussel liquid and wine and cook until it thickens. Add the mussels, season to taste and heat gently.

Cook the spaghetti in a large pan of boiling salted water for 8–10 minutes, or according to the packet instructions, until al dente. Drain. Transfer to a warmed dish, pour on the sauce and sprinkle with parsley to garnish.

Serves 4

Trenette with Anchovies and Tomatoes

4–6 tablespoons olive oil

2 garlic cloves, crushed

2 large onions, finely chopped

1 red pepper, skinned, deseeded and cut into strips

425 g (14 oz) can chopped plum tomatoes

40 g (1½ oz) can anchovies, drained and chopped

pinch of sugar

500 g (1 lb) trenette

8 tablespoons grated Parmesan cheese

salt and pepper

1 tablespoon finely chopped parsley, to garnish

Heat half of the oil in a pan and cook the garlic and onions until soft and just beginning to colour.

Add the pepper strips and cook until soft, then add the tomatoes and anchovies, season with pepper and stir in the sugar. Cook for a few minutes longer until the tomatoes and anchovies are heated through.

Meanwhile, cook the pasta in boiling salted water for about 8 minutes, or according to the packet instructions, until al dente. Drain thoroughly.

Place in a hot serving dish and stir in a little sauce, half the cheese and, if you like, the remaining oil.

Pour over the rest of the sauce just before serving, and sprinkle the chopped parsley over the top. Serve the remaining grated cheese separately.

Serves 4

Tip: To remove the skin from a pepper, place the halved or quartered pepper under a moderately hot grill until the skin starts to blacken and curl. At this point, scrape the skin off the pepper with a sharp knife.

right: spaghetti marinara

Spaghetti Marinara

300 g (10 oz) wholewheat spaghetti

4 tablespoons olive oil

1 onion, chopped

300 ml (½ pint) dry white wine

1 garlic clove, crushed

150 ml (¼ pint) double cream

2 tablespoons chopped chives

175 g (6 oz) cooked peeled prawns

250 g (8 oz) can mussels, drained

salt and pepper

grated Parmesan, to serve

Cook the spaghetti in plenty of boiling salted water for 10–12 minutes, or according to the packet instructions, until al dente. Drain, rinse with hot water and then drain thoroughly in a sieve. Leave until cold.

Meanwhile, heat 2 tablespoons of the oil in a large frying pan, add the onion and fry gently for 5 minutes, until softened. Add the wine and garlic, and simmer until reduced by one-third. Add the cream, chives, prawns and mussels to the pan. Heat through gently and season with salt and pepper to taste.

Toss the spaghetti in the remaining oil. Divide between 4 serving plates and spoon over the seafood sauce. Serve immediately, with Parmesan cheese handed separately.

Serves 4

Spaghetti with Sardines, Anchovies and Fennel

1 head fennel, quartered
8–10 tablespoons olive oil
2 garlic cloves, crushed

500 g (1 lb) sardines
2 large onions, finely sliced
1 tablespoon sultanas
1 tablespoon pine nuts
6 anchovy fillets, chopped
2 tablespoons chopped parsley
150 ml (5 fl oz) white wine or fish stock
500 g (1 lb) spaghetti
white breadcrumbs, lightly browned
salt and pepper

Cook the fennel in boiling salted water until almost tender. Drain well, reserving the cooking liquid. Chop the fennel coarsely.

Heat 3 tablespoons of the oil in a pan and add the garlic. Cook gently until golden brown, then add the sardines and cook gently for a further 10 minutes.

Meanwhile, heat another 3 tablespoons of the oil in a pan and cook the onions until they are soft and golden brown.

Add the fennel, sultanas, pine nuts, anchovies, parsley and wine or fish stock. Season lightly. Cook over a moderate heat for 10 minutes.

Cook the spaghetti in boiling salted water, to which the fennel water has been added, for 8–10 minutes, or according to the packet instructions, until al dente. Drain well and place half in an oven-to-table dish. Cover with half the sardines and a little of the onions and fennel.

Repeat the layers and sprinkle breadcrumbs and a little oil over the top. Cook in a preheated oven, 200°C (400°F), Gas Mark 6, for 20 minutes. Serve immediately, sprinkled with black pepper.

Serves 4

Tip: To prepare the sardines, bone them and remove the heads and tails. Cut each sardine into 2 or 3 pieces, depending on size, before cooking.

Linguine with Mussels in Tomato Sauce

2.5 litres (4 pints) mussels

3 tablespoons olive oil

1 onion, chopped

3 garlic cloves, crushed

750 g (1½ lb) tomatoes, skinned and
   chopped

500 g (1 lb) linguine

salt and pepper

3 tablespoons chopped parsley, to
   garnish

Prepare the mussels, discarding any
that remain open when tapped.

Scrub the mussels and remove all
the beards.

Place the mussels in a large
saucepan with 100 ml (3½ fl oz)
water, cover with a lid and cook
over a moderate heat until the
mussels open, shaking the pan
occasionally. Drain the mussels and
discard any that have not opened.
Remove the mussel shells, leaving a
few in their shells for the garnish.

Heat the olive oil in a frying pan
and add the onion and garlic. Sauté
over a medium heat until golden
and tender.

Add the chopped tomatoes,
season with salt and pepper to taste,
then cook gently over a low heat
until the mixture is thickened
and reduced.

Add the shelled mussels and
mix gently into the tomato sauce.
Simmer over a low heat for
2–3 minutes or until the mussels
are heated through.

Cook the linguine in salted
boiling water for 5 minutes,
or according to the packet
instructions, until al dente. Drain
well and gently toss with the
tomato and mussel sauce.

Transfer to a serving dish or
4 warmed plates. Sprinkle with
chopped parsley and garnish with
the reserved mussels.

Serves 4

Prawn Sauce with Sun-dried Tomatoes

8 tablespoons olive oil
350 g (12 oz) button mushrooms,
  sliced
350 g (12 oz) large shelled prawns
40 g (1½ oz) sun-dried tomatoes,
  finely chopped
2 tablespoons lemon juice
10 spring onions, sliced diagonally
3 tablespoons chopped basil
250 g (8 oz) spaghetti verde
salt and pepper

Heat the oil in a pan until almost smoking. Add the mushrooms and stir-fry for 2 minutes.

Add the prawns and sun-dried tomatoes, and stir-fry for 3 minutes.

Add the lemon juice and spring onions, and stir-fry for another 2 minutes. Stir in the basil and season to taste with salt and pepper.

Cook the pasta in boiling salted water for 8–10 minutes, or according to the packet instructions, until al dente. Drain the pasta well and toss with half the sauce. Transfer to a serving dish, spoon the remaining sauce over the top, and serve immediately.

Serves 4–6

left: prawn sauce with sun-dried
tomatoes, spaghetti alle vongole

Spaghetti alle Vongole

1 kg (2 lb) fresh clams, scrubbed
100 ml (3½ fl oz) olive oil
1 garlic clove, sliced
425 g (14 oz) tomatoes, skinned and
  mashed
425 g (14 oz) spaghetti
1 tablespoon chopped parsley
salt and pepper

Put the clams in a large pan with 100ml (3½ fl oz) water. Cook until the shells open, then remove the clams from their shells. Strain the cooking liquid and reserve.

Heat the oil in a heavy pan, add the garlic and fry gently for 5 minutes. Remove the garlic, then add the tomatoes and the reserved cooking liquid to the pan. Stir and simmer for 20 minutes.

Meanwhile, cook the spaghetti in plenty of boiling salted water for 8–10 minutes, or according to the packet instructions, until al dente. Drain the pasta, rinse with hot water and then drain thoroughly in a sieve.

Add the clams and parsley to the tomato sauce and heat through for 1 minute. Pile the spaghetti in a warmed serving dish, add the sauce and a pinch of pepper, and fold gently to mix. Serve immediately.

Serves 4

Savoury Baked Macaroni

2 tablespoons oil
1 large onion, finely chopped
2 garlic cloves, crushed
1 small chilli, deseeded and finely
  chopped
4 rashers bacon, derinded and
  chopped
425 g (14 oz) can tomatoes
1 teaspoon sugar
250 g (8 oz) dried macaroni
50 g (2 oz) Provolone or other hard
  cheese, grated
salt

Heat the oil in a saucepan, add the onion, garlic, chilli and bacon and fry gently for 10 minutes, stirring occasionally. Add the tomatoes with their juice, the sugar, and salt to taste. Bring to the boil, stirring, cover and simmer for 20 minutes.

Cook the macaroni in boiling salted water for 8 minutes, or according to the packet instructions, until al dente and drain thoroughly.

Arrange alternate layers of pasta, sauce and cheese in an oiled ovenproof dish, finishing with cheese. Serve immediately, or cover and leave in a preheated oven, 140°C (275°F), Gas Mark 1, for 20–30 minutes to allow the flavours to blend.

Serves 3–4

season with pepper. Toss well. Beat the reserved shellfish liquid with the yogurt, stir in the parsley and pour over the pasta. Toss well. Turn the pasta into a heated dish, garnish with lemon balm or coriander and the reserved mussels in their shells and serve with Parmesan cheese, if liked.

Serves 4

Anchovy and Pine Kernel Fettuccine

Hazelnuts may be substituted for the pine kernels.

25 g (1 oz) unsalted butter
1 large onion, very finely chopped
2 garlic cloves, crushed
50 g (2 oz) pine kernels
4–6 canned anchovy fillets, drained
    and pounded to a paste
175 g (6 oz) double cream
125 g (4 oz) cream or curd cheese
375 g (12 oz) fettuccine
1 tablespoon olive oil
salt and pepper
finely chopped parsley, to garnish

Melt the butter in a large saucepan, add the onion, cover and cook gently for 10 minutes until softened but not coloured. Add the garlic and pine kernels, and cook for 5 minutes. Stir the pounded

Pasta Twists with Mussels

1 kg (2 lb) fresh mussels
150 ml (¼ pint) dry white wine
1 bouquet garni
375 g (12 oz) wholewheat twists, or
    other pasta shapes
50 g (2 oz) butter
300 g (10 oz) natural yogurt
2 tablespoons chopped parsley
salt and pepper
lemon balm or coriander, to garnish
Parmesan cheese, to serve (optional)

Wash the mussels thoroughly in several bowls of clean water and pull off the beards. Tap the mussels and discard any that do not close. Pour them in a large pan with

300ml (½ pint) water and the wine, bring to the boil, cover the pan and steam for 5–6 minutes, or until the shells have opened. Drain the mussels and reserve the cooking liquid. Discard any unopened mussels. Pour the liquid into a saucepan, add the bouquet garni, bring to the boil and boil rapidly for 10 minutes, or until reduced by about two-thirds. Discard the bouquet garni. Cut the mussels away from the shells, reserving about 8 in the shells for the garnish.

Cook the pasta in plenty of boiling salted water for 12–14 minutes, or according to the packet instructions, until al dente. Drain, rinse with hot water and drain thoroughly.

Melt the butter in the pan, add the pasta twists and mussels and anchovy fillets into 2–3 tablespoons of the cream or curd cheese, then gradually stir in the rest of the cream and mix into the cheese. When smooth, stir into the mixture in the pan and cook gently for 10 minutes.

Meanwhile, cook the fettuccine in plenty of boiling salted water for 5 minutes, or according to the packet instructions, until al dente. Drain the pasta, rinse with hot water and drain in a sieve.

Return the fettuccine to the rinsed out pan with the oil, stirring until thoroughly coated. Tip the pasta into the cream sauce, mix thoroughly and season with salt and pepper, if necessary. Transfer the mixture to a hot serving dish, sprinkle with parsley, to garnish and serve.

Serves 4

Smoked Haddock with Red Pepper Sauce

500 g (1 lb) smoked haddock fillets
600 ml (1 pint) milk
2 tablespoons olive oil

3 shallots, finely chopped
2–3 garlic cloves, finely chopped
2 large red peppers, cored, deseeded and finely sliced
4 tablespoons soured cream
125 g (4 oz) low-fat soft cheese
1 tablespoon finely chopped tarragon
¼–½ teaspoon caster sugar (optional)
250 g (8 oz) pasta bows or shells
25 g (1 oz) butter
pepper

Rinse the haddock in cold water, then pour boiling water over it and leave for 2 minutes. Rinse again, then put into a pan, cover with the milk and bring to the boil. Reduce the heat and simmer gently for 10–15 minutes until the fish flakes easily. Strain, reserving the milk, and leave the fish until cool enough to handle easily.

Heat the oil in another pan, add the shallots and garlic and fry

gently for 5 minutes until softened. Add the peppers and cook gently for 5–6 minutes, stirring occasionally to prevent them sticking.

Stir 125 ml (4 fl oz) of the strained milk into the soured cream, then mix in the cheese. Add another tablespoon or so of milk if the mixture seems very thick; it should be the consistency of double cream. Purée the peppers with the cheese mixture in a blender or food processor or simply stir the cream into the peppers, but do make sure that the peppers have been very finely sliced. Return to the pan and add the tarragon and pepper. Taste the sauce, and add a little sugar if necessary. Simmer gently.

Bring the remaining milk to the boil in a large pan. Add the pasta and boil for 10–12 minutes, or according to the packet instructions, until al dente.

While the pasta is cooking, skin, bone and flake the fish. Add the sauce, stirring well to mix. Strain the pasta, return to the pan with half the butter and toss to coat. Over a medium–high heat, whisk the remaining butter into the sauce. Pile the pasta into a hot serving dish, pour the sauce over and serve at once.

Serves 4–6

---

left: smoked haddock with red pepper sauce
right: smoked cod jumble

Smoked Cod Jumble

250 g (8 oz) macaroni
75 g (3 oz) butter
375 g (12 oz) smoked cod or haddock
   fillet, skinned and cut into chunks
4 tomatoes, chopped
6 spring onions, trimmed and
   chopped
salt and pepper

Cook the macaroni in plenty of boiling salted water for 8–10 minutes, or according to the packet instructions, until al dente. Drain thoroughly.

Melt the butter in a saucepan. Add the fish, cover and cook very gently for 10 minutes, or until the fish is tender. Remove the lid, add the cooked macaroni, chopped tomato and spring onions, and season carefully. Stir the mixture lightly to avoid breaking up the fish, and reheat thoroughly. Serve with hot toast.

Serves 4

Pasta with Smoked Salmon and Basil

6 tablespoons full-fat soft cheese, at
 room temperature
6 tablespoons natural yogurt
375 g (12 oz) smoked salmon, cut
 into short strips
2 tablespoons finely chopped basil
375 g (12 oz) pasta shells or bows
2 tablespoons walnut oil
freshly ground nutmeg
salt and pepper
basil sprigs, to garnish

Mash the cheese with the yogurt
until smooth and creamy, then add
the smoked salmon strips and basil
and mix well. Leave to stand while
cooking the pasta.

Cook the pasta in plenty of
boiling salted water for 10–12
minutes, or according to the packet
instructions, until al dente. Drain,
rinse with hot water and drain
thoroughly in a sieve.

Return the pasta to the rinsed-out
pan. Add the walnut oil and stir the
pasta over a medium heat until
thoroughly coated with the oil.
Pour in the cheese and yogurt
mixture and stir for another 2–3
minutes until very hot. Season
generously with pepper and
nutmeg, garnish with the basil and
serve immediately.

Serves 4

Fresh Pasta with Crab and Courgettes

125 g (4 oz) courgettes, trimmed
25 g (1 oz) butter
1 garlic clove, crushed
125 g (4 oz) fresh pasta, such as
 green and white linguine
75 g (3 oz) white crab meat
1 teaspoon lemon juice
salt and pepper
To garnish:
lemon wedges
sprig of parsley

Cut the courgettes into slices
lengthways, then again lengthways
to make thin strips. Melt the
butter in a pan, add the garlic and
cook for 2 minutes. Add the
courgettes to the pan and cook
for a further 3 minutes, stirring
frequently.

Meanwhile, cook the pasta in
plenty of boiling salted water for
3–4 minutes, or according to the
packet instructions, until al dente.
Drain, rinse with hot water and
drain thoroughly in a sieve.

Add the pasta to the pan with the
courgettes, then add the crab,
lemon juice and season with salt
and pepper. Stir well, reheat gently
to make sure the crab is heated
through and serve garnished with
lemon wedges and parsley sprigs.

Serves 4

Tagliarini with Tuna

200 g (7 oz) can tuna fish, in oil
1 garlic clove, crushed
2 tablespoons chopped parsley
250 g (8 oz) ripe tomatoes, skinned
 and chopped
150 ml (¼ pint) chicken stock
375 g (12 oz) dried tagliarini
salt and pepper

Drain the oil from the tuna into a
pan, add the garlic and heat gently
for 2 minutes. Add the parsley and
tomatoes and cook until the
tomatoes begin to soften. Flake the
tuna and add to the pan with the
stock, and salt and pepper to taste.
Simmer while cooking the pasta.

Cook the pasta in boiling salted
water for 10–12 minutes, or
according to the packet
instructions, until al dente. Then
drain well. Turn into a warmed
serving dish. Add the sauce, toss
and serve immediately.

Serves 4

*right: fresh pasta with crab and
courgettes*

one-third of the vegetable mixture. Repeat these layers, and sprinkle the breadcrumbs and cheese on top.

Cook in a preheated oven, 200°C (400°F), Gas Mark 6, for 30–35 minutes, until the pasta is tender and the top is browned.

Serves 4

Italian Fish Salad

250 g (8 oz) pasta shells, penne, or
   short-cut shapes
500 g (1 lb) squid, cleaned
5 tablespoons olive oil
3 garlic cloves, crushed
1 kg (2 lb) fresh mussels
125 g (4 oz) cooked peeled prawns
6 celery sticks, sliced, tops reserved
1 green pepper, cored, deseeded and
   cut into strips
1 red pepper, cored, deseeded and
   cut into strips
lettuce leaves, to serve
salt and pepper
Dressing:
8 tablespoons olive oil
2 tablespoons lemon juice
1 teaspoon caster sugar (optional)
2 teaspoons finely chopped parsley
To garnish:
whole cooked prawns
celery tops

Cook the pasta in plenty of boiling salted water for 10–12 minutes, or according to the packet instructions, until al dente. Drain, rinse in hot water and drain again.

Seafood and Vegetable Lasagne

2 tablespoons vegetable oil
4 tomatoes, skinned, deseeded and
   chopped
2 courgettes, sliced
125 g (4 oz) button mushrooms,
   sliced
9 sheets wholewheat or lasagne verde
1 quantity Seafood Sauce (see
   page 17)
2 tablespoons fresh white or brown
   breadcrumbs
2 tablespoons grated Cheddar cheese

Heat 1 tablespoon of the oil in a frying pan, add the tomatoes and courgettes and fry for 3–4 minutes until the mixture begins to thicken. Stir in the mushrooms and remove from the heat.

Feed the lasagne into a large saucepan of boiling salted water one sheet at a time, keeping the water boiling. Reduce the heat slightly and cook for 10–12 minutes, stirring occasionally, until the lasagne is al dente. Drain the lasagne well, rinse with hot water, then separate the sheets and place on a plate.

Grease a shallow ovenproof dish. Spread one-third of the Seafood Sauce over the base of the dish, cover with 3 sheets of lasagne and

Cut the squid body into rings. Reserve the tentacles. Rinse and dry on kitchen paper. Sit a large frying pan over a high heat. Put in the squid rings and cook, stirring, for 3–4 minutes – a pink liquid will collect which can be discarded. Remove the squid and reserve. Wipe the pan with kitchen paper. Heat 1 tablespoon of the oil and fry one crushed garlic clove, without browning. Return the squid and reserved tentacles to the pan and cook for 3 minutes, then transfer to a bowl.

Wash the mussels thoroughly in several bowls of clean water and pull off the beards. Tap the mussels and discard any that do not close.

Place the frying pan over a high heat again, then add the mussels with another crushed garlic clove. Cover and cook over a high heat, shaking the pan from time to time for 5 minutes or until the mussel shells have opened. Discard any that do not open. Remove the mussels from their shells, reserving a few in their shells for the garnish.

Mix together the squid, shelled mussels and peeled prawns and season lightly with salt and pepper. Make the dressing: mix together the remaining garlic clove, olive oil, lemon juice, sugar, if using, parsley and seasoning and pour over the fish. Add the celery, peppers and pasta shapes, and toss well. Line a bowl or platter with lettuce leaves, and spoon in the mixture. Garnish with the reserved unshelled mussels, the whole prawns and the celery tops.

Serves 6

Smoked Trout and Pasta Salad

175 g (6 oz) pasta shells or bows
1 tablespoon olive oil
40 g (1½ oz) flaked almonds
250 g (8 oz) broccoli, cut in florets
125 g (4 oz) frozen peas
250 g (8 oz) smoked trout fillets
125 g (4 oz) cherry tomatoes, halved
salt and pepper
few sprigs of dill or parsley, to garnish
well-flavoured mayonnaise, to serve

Cook the pasta in boiling salted water for 10–12 minutes, or according to packet instructions, until al dente. Drain in a colander and cool under cold running water. Drain thoroughly.

Meanwhile, heat the oil in a small pan. Add the almonds and cook, stirring, for about 1 minute until browned. Tip into a big salad bowl.

Add the pasta to the bowl and toss to mix with the oil and almonds.

Add the broccoli and peas to a large pan of boiling water. Blanch for 1 minute, then drain and cool under cold running water. Drain thoroughly.

Flake the trout fillets and add to the pasta with the broccoli, peas and cherry tomatoes. Season with a little salt and pepper. Serve with the mayonnaise drizzled over and garnished with dill or parsley.

Serves 4

Oriental Crab and Pasta Salad

175 g (6 oz) dried egg vermicelli
4 tablespoons groundnut or corn oil
2 garlic cloves, crushed
1–2 fresh red chillies, to taste, deseeded and finely chopped
6 spring onions, finely chopped
50 g (2 oz) dark crab meat
4 tablespoons soy sauce
2 tablespoons lime or lemon juice, or to taste
250 g (8 oz) white crab meat, flaked
¼ large cucumber, skinned and cut into matchstick strips
salt and pepper
lettuce leaves, shredded, to serve
sprigs of parsley, to garnish

Bring a large saucepan of salted water to the boil. Add the vermicelli, stir and bring back to the boil. Reduce the heat and boil, uncovered, for 5 minutes, or according to packet instructions, stirring occasionally, until al dente.

Drain the vermicelli and rinse it briefly under cold running water to prevent over cooking. Drain it again well and leave to cool.

Heat 1 tablespoon of the oil in a small frying pan. Add the garlic, chillies and half the spring onions and stir-fry for 1–2 minutes until the mixture gives off a spicy aroma. Transfer to a bowl and leave to cool.

Put the dark crab meat in the bottom of a large bowl. Add the garlic, chilli and spring onion mixture, the remaining oil, the soy sauce and the lime or lemon juice. Whisk vigorously to make a smooth dressing. When the pasta is cold, add it to the bowl of dressing and stir well until the strands of vermicelli are evenly coated. Add the flaked white crab meat, the remaining spring onions and the cucumber and fold them together gently. Add salt and pepper to taste and more lime or lemon juice, if liked. Cover the bowl tightly and place in the refrigerator to chill for 30 minutes–1 hour.

To serve, line 4 individual plates with shredded lettuce leaves. Divide the salad between them and garnish with the parsley sprigs.

Serves 4

Pasta Bows with Spinach and Prawns

500 g (1 lb) cooked peeled prawns, defrosted and thoroughly dried if frozen
375 g (12 oz) pasta bows
250 g (8 oz) spinach leaves, washed, dried and torn into pieces
salt and pepper
Marinade:
1 tablespoon coriander seeds
6 tablespoons olive oil
3–4 garlic cloves, crushed
2 tablespoons dry white wine

2 tablespoons Pernod
finely grated rind and juice of 1 lime
salt and pepper

First make the marinade: dry fry the coriander seeds in a non-stick frying pan for a few seconds until they give off a spicy aroma. Transfer them to a mortar and crush finely with a pestle. Place in a large bowl with the remaining ingredients. Whisk well to mix them together.

Stir the prawns into the marinade, coating them well. Cover and leave to marinate in a cold place for 3–4 hours, stirring occasionally.

Bring a large saucepan of salted water to the boil. Add the pasta, stir and bring back to the boil. Reduce the heat and boil for 10–12 minutes, or according to the packet instructions, stirring occasionally, until al dente.

Drain the pasta well and turn into a warm bowl. Add the prawns and marinade and toss them together well. Add the spinach and toss again. Adjust the seasoning if necessary. Divide the pasta equally between 4 warm soup plates and serve at once.

Serves 4

above: pasta bows with spinach and prawns

Baked Macaroni with Fresh Prawns

100 g (3½ oz) butter
175 g (6 oz) button mushrooms, sliced
250 g (8 oz) cooked peeled prawns
2 tablespoons warmed brandy
40 g (1½ oz) Parmesan cheese, grated
250 g (8 oz) short macaroni
salt and pepper
sprigs of basil, to garnish
Béchamel sauce:
25 g (1 oz) butter
25 g (1 oz) flour
300 ml (½ pint) milk
pinch of ground nutmeg
40g (1½ oz) Parmesan cheese, grated

Make 300 ml (½ pint) béchamel sauce (see page 36). Keep warm. Heat half the butter in a pan and cook the mushrooms until tender. Season with salt and pepper to taste.

Add the prawns and heat through, then pour on the warmed brandy and set alight. When the flames have subsided, stir in half the cheese and check the seasoning.

Meanwhile, cook the pasta in boiling salted water for 8–10 minutes, or according to the packet instructions, until al dente. Drain well. Check the seasoning of the béchamel sauce and add a pinch of nutmeg and the cheese.

Place a third of the macaroni in a buttered oven dish and spread with half the mushroom mixture. Repeat the layers, ending with macaroni.

Cover with the béchamel sauce. Heat the remaining butter in a pan and, when it is lightly coloured, pour it over the top. Bake in a preheated oven, 200°C (400°F), Gas Mark 6, for about 20 minutes until golden brown. Garnish with basil.

Serves 4

Seafood Cannelloni

2 celery sticks, chopped
2 carrots, chopped
600 ml (1 pint) milk
1 onion, quartered
3 peppercorns
1 bay leaf
50 g (2 oz) butter
50 g (2 oz) flour
1 tablespoon chopped dill
2 tablespoons snipped chives
250 g (8 oz) recipe quantity
    Homemade Egg Pasta (see page 8)
2 tablespoons dried breadcrumbs
salt and pepper
prawns and dill sprigs, to garnish
Filling:
15 g (½ oz) butter
2 spring onions, chopped
50 g (2 oz) button mushrooms, finely chopped
150 ml (¼ pint) dry white wine
125 g (4 oz) cooked peeled prawns
125 g (4 oz) cooked or canned crab meat, flaked
125 g (4 oz) Cheddar cheese, grated
4 tablespoons grated Parmesan

Put the celery and carrots in a pan with the milk, onion, peppercorns and bay leaf. Bring to the boil, remove from the heat and cool. Strain and reserve the milk.

Melt the butter in a pan, add the flour and cook for 2 minutes, stirring constantly. Gradually add the reserved milk, bring to the boil and cook for 2 minutes, stirring, until smooth and thickened. Stir in the dill and chives and season.

For the filling: melt the butter in a pan, add the spring onions and mushrooms and cook for 1 minute. Add the wine and boil to reduce to 1–2 tablespoons.

Take off the heat, stir in one-quarter of the sauce and mix. Add the prawns, crab meat and season. Stir in the cheeses until melted.

Roll out the pasta dough thinly. Cut into 8 x 10 cm (3 x 4 inch) sheets and cook in boiling salted water for 1 minute. Drain well and lay on clean tea towels.

Divide the seafood filling between the pasta sheets and roll up from the shorter side. Arrange in a single layer, seam side down, in a lightly greased ovenproof dish. Spoon over the remaining sauce and sprinkle with the breadcrumbs.

Cook in a preheated oven, 200°C (400°F), Gas Mark 6, for 15–20 minutes, until golden. Garnish with prawns and dill sprigs.

Serves 4

Spaghetti with Prawns and Vodka

3 tablespoons olive oil

1 small onion, finely chopped

200 g (7 oz) can tomatoes

1 garlic clove, crushed

3 tablespoons dry white wine
(optional)

1 teaspoon tomato purée

few sprigs of rosemary and basil
leaves

250–300 g (8–10 oz) spaghetti

15 g (½ oz) butter

250 g (8 oz) cooked peeled prawns,
thoroughly defrosted and dried if
frozen

175 g (6 oz) small whole button
mushrooms

4 tablespoons vodka

75 ml (3 fl oz) double cream

salt and pepper

To garnish:

few unpeeled prawns

basil leaves

Heat half the oil in a heavy pan.
Add the onion and cook it gently,
stirring frequently, until softened –
about 5 minutes. Add the tomatoes
and garlic and stir the tomatoes well
to break them up, pressing them
against the side of the pan if
necessary. Add the wine, if using,
the tomato purée, rosemary and
basil leaves. Season with salt and
pepper to taste. Simmer, uncovered,
for about 15 minutes, stirring until

the sauce is reduced to a thick
purée. Remove the pan from the
heat. Bring a large pan of salted
water to the boil. Add the spaghetti,
stir and bring back to the boil.
Reduce the heat slightly and boil,
uncovered, for 8–10 minutes, or
according to the packet
instructions, stirring occasionally
until al dente.

Meanwhile, heat the remaining
oil in a heavy frying pan. Add the
butter and heat until sizzling. Add
the prawns and mushrooms, stirring

well. Pour in the vodka, increase the
heat and cook, stirring constantly,
until all the liquid has evaporated.
Add the tomato sauce and cream
and stir until well blended and
heated through.

Drain the spaghetti well and
transfer it to a warm bowl. Pour
over the sauce and serve at once,
garnished with a few unpeeled
prawns and basil leaves.

Serves 4

Vegetables and Salads

Tomato Tagliatelle with Vegetable Sauce

500 g (1 lb) fresh red tagliatelle
2 tablespoons vegetable oil
15 g (½ oz) butter
2 onions, sliced

2 garlic cloves, crushed
500 g (1 lb) courgettes, trimmed and
 finely sliced
1 green pepper, cored, deseeded and
 finely sliced
2 large tomatoes, skinned and
 chopped
250 g (8 oz) button mushrooms,
 sliced
2 tablespoons chopped parsley
salt and pepper

Topping:
150 g (5 oz) cottage cheese, sieved
25 g (1 oz) Cheddar cheese, grated
2 tablespoons chopped parsley
2 tablespoons natural yogurt

Cook the tagliatelle in a large pan of lightly salted boiling water for 3–4 minutes, or according to the packet instructions, until al dente. Drain the pasta, run hot water through it to prevent it from becoming sticky, and drain it again. Return it to the pan and keep it warm.

To make the sauce, heat the oil and butter in a saucepan and fry the onions over a moderate heat for 3 minutes, stirring once or twice. Add the garlic, courgettes and green pepper and fry for 3 minutes. Add the tomatoes and mushrooms, stir well, cover the pan and simmer for 10 minutes, or until the vegetables are just tender. Season with salt and pepper and stir in the parsley.

To make the topping: lightly mix together the cottage cheese, Cheddar, parsley and yogurt, and season with pepper.

Turn the tagliatelle into a heated serving dish, pour on the sauce and toss with two spoons to distribute it evenly. Spoon the cheese topping into the centre and serve at once.

Serves 4

Mandarin Noodles

1 small cucumber, halved lengthways

250 g (8 oz) dried noodles or
   wholewheat spaghetti

125 g (4 oz) beansprouts

4 spring onions, white part only,
   finely sliced

125 g (4 oz) cold roast pork,
   shredded (optional)

salt and pepper

Dressing:

4 tablespoons groundnut or
   sunflower oil

1 tablespoon sesame oil

2 tablespoons light soy sauce

1 teaspoon sugar (optional)

To garnish:

1 teaspoon sesame seeds

spring onion tassels

Scoop out the cucumber seeds and cut the flesh into 4 cm (1½ inch) lengths and then into matchstick pieces. Sprinkle with salt and leave for 15 minutes.

Cook the noodles or spaghetti in boiling, salted water for 5 minutes, or according to the packet instructions, until al dente. Drain, refresh in cold water and drain.

Dry-fry the sesame seeds for the garnish in a frying pan until lightly toasted, and reserve.

To make the dressing: mix together the groundnut or sunflower and sesame oils with the soy sauce and sugar. Taste and adjust the seasoning.

Pile the noodles or spaghetti on to a serving dish. Toss lightly with the cucumber, beansprouts, sliced spring onions and pork, if using, to mix.

Pour over the prepared dressing and toss. Garnish with the spring onion tassles and sesame seeds.

Serves 6

Tagliatelle with Tomato and Basil Sauce

4 tablespoons olive oil

2 onions, chopped

1 garlic clove, crushed

500 g (1 lb) tomatoes, skinned and chopped

2 tablespoons tomato purée

1 teaspoon sugar

100 ml (3½ fl oz) dry white wine

few olives, pitted and quartered

handful of torn basil leaves

375 g (12 oz) dried tagliatelle

salt and pepper

50 g (2 oz) Parmesan cheese, shaved, to serve

Heat 3 tablespoons of the olive oil in a large frying pan. Add the onions and garlic, and sauté gently over a low heat until they are soft and slightly coloured. Stir the mixture occasionally.

Add the tomatoes, tomato purée, sugar and wine, stirring well. Cook over a gentle heat until the mixture is quite thick and reduced. Stir in the quartered olives and torn basil leaves, and season with salt and plenty of pepper to taste.

Meanwhile, add the tagliatelle to a large pan of boiling salted water. Boil rapidly for 5 minutes, or according to the packet instructions, until al dente.

Drain the tagliatelle immediately, mixing in the remaining olive oil and a generous pinch of pepper. Arrange the pasta on 4 serving plates and top with the tomato sauce, mixing it into the tagliatelle. Serve with large curls of shaved Parmesan.

Serves 4

Tagliatelle with Radicchio and Cream

Have the pan of boiling salted water ready for the pasta before you start making the sauce, plus a large, warm serving bowl, as the sauce is best served very fresh.

250 g (8 oz) radicchio

50 g (2 oz) butter

1 tablespoon olive oil

1 onion, very finely chopped

150 ml (¼ pint) double cream

250–300 g (8–10 oz) fresh tagliatelle

50 g (2 oz) Parmesan cheese, freshly grated

salt and pepper

Shred the radicchio finely, reserving a few small, curly inner leaves for the garnish. Melt the butter with the oil in a large, heavy saucepan. Add the onion and cook gently, stirring frequently, for about 10 minutes until it is softened.

Add the shredded radicchio and cook, stirring over a moderate heat, until it wilts and begins to turn brown. Add salt to taste and plenty of pepper. Stir in the cream and heat through.

Plunge the pasta into a pan of boiling salted water, stir and bring back to the boil. Reduce the heat and boil, uncovered, for 3–4 minutes or according to the packet instructions, stirring occasionally, until al dente.

Drain the tagliatelle well. Taste the sauce and adjust the seasoning if necessary. Place the tagliatelle in a warm serving bowl, pour over the sauce and add the grated Parmesan cheese. Toss quickly to combine. Serve at once, garnished with the reserved radicchio leaves.

Serves 4

Conchiglie with Chickpeas and Tahini

2 tablespoons olive oil

2 garlic cloves, crushed

2 x 425 g (14 oz) cans chickpeas

2 tablespoons tahini paste

1 tablespoon finely chopped parsley, plus a few sprigs, to garnish

juice of ½ lemon, to taste

375–425 g (12–14 oz) dried large conchiglie (pasta shells)

salt and pepper

Heat the oil in a heavy pan, add the

garlic and fry very gently until it is just beginning to change colour. Drain the chickpeas and pour 4 tablespoons of the liquid into the pan. Add the chickpeas, tahini, parsley, lemon juice, salt and pepper and 300 ml (½ pint) cold water. Bring slowly to the boil, stirring, and simmer for 10 minutes. Meanwhile, bring a pan of salted water to the boil, add the pasta, stir and bring to the boil. Reduce the

heat and boil for 10–12 minutes, or according to the packet instructions, stirring occasionally, until al dente.

Transfer the chickpea mixture to a blender and blend it to a purée, or push it through a sieve. Rinse out the pan, return the purée to it and heat it through. If the sauce is a little too thick, add a few tablespoons of water until it is the right consistency for pouring over

the pasta. Adjust the seasoning.

Drain the pasta well and turn into a warm bowl. Add the sauce and toss together gently. Serve garnished with the parsley sprigs.

Serves 4

above: conchiglie with chickpeas and tahini

Tagliatelle with Cheese and Walnuts

250 g (8 oz) fresh tagliatelle
125 g (4 oz) cream cheese
125 g (4 oz) soured cream
50 g (2 oz) walnuts, finely chopped
salt and pepper
black grapes, halved and pips
   removed, to garnish

Chickpea Hotpot with Spaghetti

250 g (8 oz) chickpeas, soaked
   overnight
1 aubergine
3 tablespoons vegetable oil
1 onion, finely sliced
12 garlic cloves, crushed
2–3 teaspoons garam masala
600 ml (1 pint) tomato juice
1 teaspoon yeast extract
50 g (2 oz) unsalted peanuts
¼ teaspoon sugar
375 g (12 oz) spaghetti
salt and pepper
1 tablespoon chopped fresh parsley,
   to garnish

Drain the chickpeas and rinse, then place in a saucepan, cover with cold water and bring to the boil. (You can add 1 teaspoon of the oil with the water, if you like – it helps prevent it boiling over.) Cook rapidly for 10 minutes, then reduce the heat and simmer for 40 minutes, or until the chickpeas are soft. Drain and set aside.

Slice the aubergine and place in a colander. Sprinkle with salt and leave for 10–20 minutes, then rinse, drain and dry on kitchen paper.

Heat the oil in a large pan, add the onion and fry gently for 5 minutes. Add the aubergine and garlic and cook for 2 minutes. Add the garam masala and cook for 2 minutes. Add the chickpeas, tomato juice, yeast extract, nuts, sugar, salt and pepper. Stir, bring to the boil, cover and simmer for 45 minutes.

Meanwhile, cook the spaghetti in boiling salted water for 8–10 minutes, or according to the packet instructions, until al dente. Drain well and put on a serving dish.

Check the hotpot seasoning, pour over the spaghetti and sprinkle with the chopped parsley. Serve immediately.

Serves 4

Bring a large pan of salted water to the boil and add the tagliatelle. Cook for about 3 minutes, or according to the packet instructions, until al dente. Strain into a colander.

Put the cream cheese, soured cream and walnuts into the warm pan and stir over a low heat, adding a little salt and plenty of pepper.

When the cheese and cream are beginning to melt, tip in the cooked tagliatelle and shake the pan to coat the pasta thoroughly.

Serve on warmed dishes, garnished with the black grapes.

Serves 3

left: chickpea hotpot with spaghetti
right: mushroom ravioli

Mushroom Ravioli

2 tablespoons olive oil

1 onion, finely chopped

1–2 garlic cloves, crushed

500 g (1 lb) mushrooms, finely
  chopped

200 g (7 oz) ricotta cheese

1 egg, beaten

2–3 tablespoons white breadcrumbs

1 recipe quantity Homemade Egg
  Pasta dough (see page 8)

75 g (3 oz) butter

salt and pepper

50 g (2 oz) Parmesan cheese, grated

Heat the oil, add the onion and garlic, and cook gently until soft and lightly coloured. Add the mushrooms and continue to cook gently until the mushrooms are soft and any liquid has evaporated.

Remove from the heat, beat in the ricotta and egg and sufficient breadcrumbs to give a firm mixture. Season with salt and pepper to taste.

Roll out the pasta dough thinly and cut out 6 cm (2 ½ inch) rounds. Place a portion of the mixture on each, brush around the edge of the dough with cold water, fold over and seal. Alternatively, cut out 2.5 cm (1 inch) square or round shapes, place the filling in the centre, brush around the edge of the dough with cold water, top with a matching shape and seal.

Cook a few ravioli at a time for 4–5 minutes in boiling salted water. They are cooked when they rise to the surface. Remove with a draining spoon, drain well. Cover and keep hot in a serving dish until all the ravioli are cooked. Just before serving, heat the butter in a pan until it is a golden brown, and pour immediately over the ravioli. Sprinkle some Parmesan over the top and serve the rest separately. Serve hot with freshly ground pepper.

Serves 4

Flamed Tagliatelle with Yogurt

375 g (12 oz) wholewheat tagliatelle, or other pasta shapes
50 g (2 oz) butter
3 tablespoons brandy
150 ml (¼ pint) natural yogurt
60 g (2½ oz) Parmesan cheese, grated
salt and pepper
50 g (2 oz) walnut halves, to garnish

Cook the tagliatelle in plenty of boiling salted water for 6 minutes, or according to the packet instructions, until al dente. Drain, refresh in hot water, and drain thoroughly again.

Melt the butter in a pan and toss the tagliatelle to coat well. Pour on the brandy, stir well and light it, to burn off the alcohol.

Stir in the yogurt and cheese, and season with pepper. Garnish with the walnuts and serve at once.

Serves 4

Spaghetti with Cheese and Almond Sauce

375 g (12 oz) buckwheat spaghetti
25 g (1 oz) butter
2 tablespoons chopped parsley
salt
Sauce:
125 g (4 oz) ground almonds
175 g (6 oz) cottage cheese, sieved
50 g (2 oz) Parmesan cheese, grated
300 g (10 oz) natural yogurt
2 tablespoons olive oil
pinch of grated nutmeg
pinch of ground cinnamon
8 tablespoons blanched almonds, toasted
pepper
1 tablespoon chopped parsley, to garnish

Cook the spaghetti in plenty of boiling salted water for 8–10 minutes, or according to the packet instructions, until al dente. Drain, return the spaghetti to the pan, toss it in the butter and parsley, cover and keep hot.

Make the sauce: mix all the ingredients together except the toasted almonds and season.

Turn the spaghetti into a heated serving dish. Stir the toasted almonds into the sauce, pour over the spaghetti and toss well. Garnish with the chopped parsley and serve.

Serves 4

Sliced Courgettes with Pasta

1 tablespoon butter
1 garlic clove, halved
5 courgettes, finely sliced
250 g (8 oz) tagliatelle
salt and pepper

Melt a little butter in a large frying pan and sauté the garlic.

Remove the garlic when it becomes golden brown, and gently cook the courgettes in the butter. Add salt and pepper to taste and continue to fry the courgettes until they are browned but not dry. Keep them hot.

Meanwhile, cook the tagliatelle in a deep pan of boiling salted water for 5 minutes, or according to the packet instructions, until al dente. Drain the pasta and return it to the pan.

Tip the courgettes, with their butter, over the pasta and serve immediately. Traditionally, this dish is served with a grind of pepper.

Serves 2–3

right: sliced courgettes with pasta

Pasta Twists with Broccoli Spears

375 g (12 oz) pasta twists, bows or
   other shapes
500 g (1 lb) broccoli spears
1 tablespoon olive oil
15 g (½ oz) butter
1 small onion, finely chopped
40 g (1½ oz) walnuts, roughly
   chopped

40 g (1½ oz) anchovy fillets, chopped
1 tablespoon chopped parsley
25 g (1 oz) Parmesan cheese, grated
salt and pepper

Cook the pasta in plenty of boiling
salted water for 10–12 minutes,
or according to the packet
instructions, until al dente. Drain
immediately, refresh in hot water,
and then drain once more.

Blanch the broccoli by cooking
it in boiling salted water for
5 minutes. Drain, and plunge at
once into cold water to prevent
further cooking. Drain again.

Heat the oil with the butter and
fry the onion over a low heat for
10 minutes, stirring occasionally.
Stir in the walnuts, anchovies and
broccoli and cook slowly over a
gentle heat for 3–4 minutes.

Stir in the pasta and heat
through. Remove from the heat,
add the parsley, season well with
pepper and stir in the cheese. Serve
at once. A green salad makes a good
accompaniment.

Serves 4

Tortellini with Spinach and Herb Sauce

50 g (2 oz) butter
250 g (8 oz) frozen leaf spinach,
  thawed and chopped
pinch of grated nutmeg
375 g (12 oz) fresh tortellini
125 g (4 oz) curd cheese
2 tablespoons single cream
2 teaspoons snipped chives
1 teaspoon chopped parsley
50 g (2 oz) Parmesan cheese, grated
salt and pepper

Heat the butter in a large frying pan, add the spinach and toss thoroughly. Add the nutmeg and season with salt and pepper to taste. Cook for about 2 minutes, stirring constantly, until tender.

Meanwhile, cook the tortellini in boiling salted water for 4 minutes, or according to the packet instructions, until al dente. Drain well and return to the pan.

Stir in the curd cheese, cream, chives, parsley and half of the Parmesan cheese, then fold in the cooked spinach. Spoon into a heated serving dish and sprinkle with the remaining Parmesan cheese to serve.

Serves 4

Spaghetti with Saffron

Freshly grated Parmesan can be served with this simple dish. It tastes really good, but if you prefer the subtlety of the saffron flavour it is better to serve it without the cheese.

425 g (14 oz) spaghetti
large pinch of saffron threads
2 tablespoons butter
½ large onion, very finely chopped
50 g (2 oz) dark crab meat
150 ml (¼ pint) extra thick double
  cream
salt and pepper

Bring a large saucepan of salted water to the boil. Add the spaghetti, stir and bring back to the boil. Reduce the heat and boil, uncovered, for 8–10 minutes or according to the packet instructions, stirring occasionally, until al dente.

Meanwhile, put the saffron threads in a heatproof bowl. Stir in 2 tablespoons of the pasta cooking water and leave the saffron to soak. Melt the butter in a heavy saucepan, add the onion and cook very gently, stirring frequently, until it is golden. Remove the pan from the heat. Strain in the saffron liquid. Pour in the cream, stirring well to blend the ingredients.

Drain the spaghetti well and turn it into a warm bowl. Reheat the saffron sauce quickly. Season with salt and pepper to taste and pour the sauce over the spaghetti, tossing it well. Serve at once.

Serves 4

left: pasta twists with broccoli spears
above: tortellini with spinach and herb sauce

Tortellini with Chicory

4 tablespoons olive oil

1 large onion, finely sliced

1 garlic clove, finely chopped

500 g (1 lb) chicory, finely sliced

500 g (1 lb) tomatoes, skinned and chopped

2 tablespoons chopped basil

1 tablespoon chopped fresh thyme or ½ teaspoon dried marjoram

500 g (1 lb) fresh tortellini

4 tablespoons chopped parsley, to garnish

Heat the oil in a large saucepan over a low heat. Put in the onion and garlic and soften them.

Mix in the chicory, tomatoes, basil, thyme, marjoram and tortellini. Cover and cook over a low heat for 10–12 minutes, or until the tortellini is tender. Serve sprinkled with parsley.

Serves 4

Variation:
Use 500 g (1 lb) fresh ravioli instead of the tortellini.

Hot Buttons and Bows

375 g (12 oz) pasta bows

4 tablespoons oil

25 g (1 oz) butter

375 g (12 oz) button mushrooms, trimmed

2 garlic cloves, crushed

4 tablespoons chopped parsley

rind of 1 lemon

salt and pepper

Cook the pasta in boiling salted water for 10–12 minutes, or according to the packet instructions, until al dente.

Meanwhile, heat the oil and butter in a frying pan, add the mushrooms and fry for 3 minutes. Add the garlic, half the parsley and salt and pepper to taste, and cook for a further 2 minutes. Cut fine strips of rind from the lemon with a potato peeler. Chop it roughly and mix it with the remaining parsley.

Drain the pasta thoroughly and put into a heatproof salad bowl. Pour the mushrooms and juices over the pasta and toss lightly together. Sprinkle the lemon and parsley mixture over the salad and serve immediately.

Serves 6

left: hot buttons and bows
right: spaghetti with almond sauce

Spaghetti with Almond Sauce

375 g (12 oz) buckwheat spaghetti
25 g (1 oz) butter
2 tablespoons chopped parsley
Sauce:
125 g (4 oz) ground almonds
175 g (6 oz) cottage cheese, sieved
50 g (2 oz) Parmesan cheese, grated
300 ml (½ pint) natural yogurt
2 tablespoons olive oil

pinch of grated nutmeg
pinch of ground cinnamon
8 tablespoons blanched almonds,
    toasted
salt and pepper
1 tablespoon chopped parsley, to
    garnish

Cook the spaghetti in plenty of
boiling salted water for about
12 minutes, or according to the
packet instructions, until al dente.
Drain, refresh in hot water, and
drain again. Return the spaghetti to
the pan, toss in the butter and
parsley, cover and keep hot.

Mix together all the sauce
ingredients except for the toasted
almonds and season.

Turn the spaghetti into a warmed
serving dish. Stir the toasted
almonds into the sauce, pour over
the spaghetti and toss well. Garnish
with the chopped parsley and serve
at once.

Serves 4

Individual Vegetable Lasagnes

2 tablespoons olive oil

2 small green peppers, cored, deseeded and finely chopped

75 g (3 oz) margarine or butter

375 g (12 oz) button mushrooms, finely sliced

2 x recipe quantity Fresh Tomato Sauce (see page 14)

50 g (2 oz) plain white (unbleached) flour or wholemeal flour

900 ml (1½ pints) milk

50 g (2 oz) Cheddar or Wensleydale cheese, grated

50 g (2 oz) Parmesan cheese, grated

¼ teaspoon grated nutmeg

about 500 g (1 lb) pre-cooked lasagne

salt and pepper

Heat the olive oil in a large, heavy-based saucepan. Add the green peppers and fry for 7–10 minutes until soft. Add 25 g (1 oz) of the margarine or butter and the mushrooms and fry for about 5 minutes. Remove the peppers and mushrooms with a slotted spoon and set aside.

Pour the tomato sauce into the juices in the pan and bring to the boil. Simmer, uncovered, until thick and reduce by one-third. Stir in the peppers and mushrooms and put to one side.

Melt the remaining margarine or butter in a clean pan, sprinkle in the flour and cook, stirring, for 1–2 minutes. Remove from the heat and beat in the milk a little at a time. Return to the heat and simmer, stirring, until smooth. Add the Cheddar or Wensleydale cheese, and half of the Parmesan, the nutmeg and salt and pepper to taste. Stir over a low heat until the cheese has melted.

Pour a layer of cheese sauce into the bottom of 6 ovenproof dishes. Put a layer of lasagne in the dishes, then pour in enough mushroom and tomato mixture to cover. Repeat these layers until all the ingredients are used, finishing with a layer of cheese sauce.

Cook in a preheated oven, 190°C (375°F), Gas Mark 5, for 30 minutes. Sprinkle with the remaining Parmesan and cook for 5 minutes.

Serves 6

Two-layer Vegetable Lasagne

250 g (8 oz) wholewheat lasagne

50 g (2 oz) butter or margarine

500 g (1 lb) carrots, grated

2 onions, finely chopped

1 garlic clove, finely chopped

4½ tablespoons wholemeal flour

600 ml (1 pint) milk

2 teaspoons coarse-grained mustard

2 boxes cress

250 g (8 oz) mushrooms, chopped

125 g (4 oz) Cheddar cheese, grated

75 g (3 oz) watercress, finely chopped

1 teaspoon Dijon mustard

orange slices and watercress, to
  garnish

Cook the lasagne in boiling salted water for 10–12 minutes, or according to the packet instructions, until al dente. Drain.

Melt one-third of the butter or margarine in a saucepan over a low heat. Stir in the carrots, 1 of the onions and the garlic. Cover and cook gently for 10 minutes. Stir in 1½ tablespoons flour and one-third of the milk. Bring to the boil, stirring, and stir until the carrots are coated with a small amount of thick sauce. Take the pan from the heat and stir in the coarse-grained mustard. Fold the cress into the carrot mixture.

Melt a further third of the butter in a saucepan over a low heat. Add the remaining onion and soften it. Raise the heat to medium. Put in the mushrooms and cook them for 1½ minutes, stirring frequently. Stir in 1½ tablespoons of flour and a further third of the milk. Bring to the boil, stirring, and stir until thickened. Take the pan off the heat and beat in one-third of the cheese and all the watercress.

Melt the remaining butter in a saucepan on a medium heat. Stir in the remaining flour and milk and bring to the boil. Simmer for 2 minutes. Beat in half the remaining cheese and the Dijon mustard.

In a large 5–8 cm (2–3 inch) deep dish, place one-third of the lasagne. Cover it with all the carrot mixture. Arrange a further third of the lasagne on top. Cover this layer with the the mushroom and watercress mixture. Top with the remaining lasagne and spread the cheese sauce over it. Sprinkle the remaining grated cheese on top. Bake in a preheated oven, 200°C (400°F), Gas Mark 6, for 30 minutes, or until the top is golden brown. Garnish with the orange slices and watercress and serve immediately.

Serves 4

Vegetable and Walnut Lasagne

750 g (1½ lb) parsnips, chopped
25 g (1 oz) butter
2 tablespoons chopped parsley
6 sheets of quick-cook lasagne
350 g (12 oz) cottage cheese
500 g (1 lb) frozen chopped spinach,
    defrosted and drained
¼ teaspoon grated nutmeg
50 g (2 oz) Emmental. sliced
25 g (1 oz) walnuts, roughly chopped
1 large tomato, halved and sliced
salt and pepper
parsley, to garnish

Cook the parsnips in boiling salted water in a 1.8 litre (3 pints) shallow flameproof dish for 12–15 minutes or until tender. Drain and mash with half the butter and the parsley.

Cover with half the lasagne, then the cottage cheese, then the remaining lasagne. Cover with the spinach and season with the nutmeg, salt and pepper to taste. Arrange the cheese slices along 2 sides of the dish.

Cook in a preheated moderate oven, 180°C (350°F), Gas Mark 4, for 30 minutes. Sprinkle the walnuts down the centre and dot with the remaining butter. Arrange the tomato slices on either side of the walnuts.

Garnish with parsley and serve hot with crusty bread.

Serves 4

Tagliatelle with Asparagus

75 g (3 oz) butter
2 garlic cloves, crushed
500 g (1 lb) thin asparagus spears, cut
    into 2.5 cm (1 inch) lengths
300 ml (½ pint) carton double cream
1 tablespoon chopped parsley
1 tablespoon chopped thyme
500 g (1 lb) fresh tagliatelle
50 g (2 oz) Parmesan cheese, grated
salt and pepper
thyme or parsley sprigs, to garnish

Heat 50 g (2 oz) of the butter in a wok or frying pan, add the garlic and asparagus and cook gently, without browning, for 7–10 minutes, until the asparagus is just tender. Add the cream, herbs, and salt and pepper to taste. Remove from the heat.

Cook the pasta for 3 minutes, or according to the packet instructions, until al dente. Drain thoroughly and turn into a warmed serving dish. Add the remaining butter and toss well.

Return the sauce to the heat for 1 minute, then pour over the pasta. Sprinkle with the Parmesan cheese and garnish with thyme or parsley sprigs. Serve immediately.

Serves 6

Spaghetti Carotese

375 g (12 oz) dried spaghetti
5 tablespoons olive oil
6 carrots, finely sliced
250 g (8 oz) tomatoes, skinned and
    chopped
3 tablespoons finely chopped basil
salt and pepper
60 g (2½ oz) Parmesan cheese,
    grated, to serve (optional)

Cook the spaghetti in boiling salted water for 8–10 minutes, or according to the packet instructions, until al dente. Drain well and keep warm.

Meanwhile, heat half of the olive oil in a pan, add the carrots and cook over a high heat until just tender. Add the chopped tomatoes, basil and salt and pepper to taste, mixing well.

Add the cooked spaghetti and toss well to mix. Transfer to a heated serving dish and serve hot, sprinkled with the Parmesan cheese if liked.

Serves 4

right: spaghetti carotese

Cappelletti with Taramasalata

375 g (12 oz) fresh spinach cappelletti, stuffed with Ricotta cheese
12 tablespoons chopped dill, plus a few sprigs to garnish

Taramasalata dressing:
125 g (4 oz) smoked cod's roe, skinned
1 teaspoon lemon juice, or to taste
1 tablespoon grated onion
250 ml (8 fl oz) single cream
salt and pepper

Cook the cappelletti in plenty of boiling, salted water for 12–14 minutes, or according to the packet instructions, until al dente. Strain and refresh in cold water, then drain thoroughly. Put into a serving bowl with the chopped dill.

Put the cod's roe into a food processor with the lemon juice and blend, or push through a sieve. When smooth, add the grated

onion and the cream. Mix for 30 seconds, then taste and season with salt and pepper as needed.

Pour the dressing over the pasta and garnish with the dill sprigs.

Serves 4

Cannelloni with Spinach Filling

750 g (1½ lb) fresh spinach, stalks
  removed
50 g (2 oz) butter
250 g (8 oz) cottage cheese, sieved
75 g (3 oz) Parmesan cheese, grated
pinch of grated nutmeg
2 eggs
12 large cannelloni tubes
25 g (1 oz) flour
300 ml (½ pint) milk
4 tablespoons bran cereal
salt and pepper

Wash the spinach, place in a large pan and cook in just the water clinging to the leaves for 5–7 minutes over a moderate heat. Stir frequently. Drain the spinach in a colander, pressing out all moisture. Chop the spinach finely.

Melt half the butter in a pan, add the spinach and stir well. Remove from the heat.

Beat the sieved cottage cheese and half the Parmesan cheese into the spinach and season with salt, pepper and nutmeg. Beat in the eggs. Set aside to cool.

Cook the cannelloni tubes in plenty of boiling salted water for 10 minutes, or according to the packet instructions, until al dente. Drain, refresh in cold water, and drain again. Dry thoroughly with kitchen paper. Set aside to cool.

Melt the remaining butter in a pan, stir in the flour, and cook for 1 minute. Remove from the heat and gradually stir in the milk, stirring constantly. Bring to the boil, season with salt and pepper and simmer for 5 minutes. Taste and adjust the seasoning if necessary.

Use a piping bag (but no nozzle) to fill the cannelloni tubes with the spinach mixture.

Place the filled cannelloni in a greased, shallow baking dish. Pour over the sauce and sprinkle with the remaining cheese mixed with the bran cereal.

Stand the dish on a baking sheet. Place in a preheated oven, 180°C (350°F), Gas Mark 4, for 35–40 minutes, or until the topping is dark brown and crusty.

Serves 4–6

left: cappelletti with taramasalata

Vermicelli with Neapolitan Sauce

4 tablespoons olive oil
2 garlic cloves, crushed
750 g (1½ lb) ripe tomatoes, skinned
  and coarsely chopped
1 sprig of basil
½ teaspoon ground cinnamon
250–300 g (8–10 oz) dried vermicelli
salt and pepper

Heat the oil in a heavy pan, add the garlic and fry gently until it begins to change colour. Add the tomatoes, basil, cinnamon and seasoning. Cover and simmer for 15 minutes, stirring frequently.

Meanwhile, bring a pan of salted water to the boil. Add the pasta, stir and bring back to the boil. Reduce the heat and boil, uncovered for 10 minutes, or according to the packet instructions, until al dente. Drain the pasta and divide between 4 warm plates. Pour the sauce over and serve.

Serves 4

coriander or parsley and mint in a food processor. Slowly add the oil, then just before serving, add the vinegar and salt and pepper to taste.

Put the pasta into a serving bowl, pour on a little dressing and toss well. Reserve some of the broccoli, red pepper, pineapple and ham for the garnish and add the remainder to the pasta.

Pour the remaining dressing over the salad and garnish with the reserved salad ingredients.

Serves 6

Insalata Delicata

200 g (7 oz) dried pasta shells

250 g (8 oz) cooked chicken breast, skinned and cut into thin slivers

125 g (4 oz) cooked peeled prawns, defrosted and thoroughly dried if frozen

1 ripe avocado

salt and pepper

lettuce leaves, to serve

tarragon sprigs, to garnish

Mayonnaise:

1 egg yolk

½ teaspoon Dijon mustard

150 ml (¼ pint) groundnut or corn oil

2 teaspoons tarragon vinegar

2 teaspoons chopped tarragon

Bring a large saucepan of salted water to the boil. Add the pasta shells, stir and bring back to the boil. Reduce the heat and boil,

Four Seasons Pasta Salad

250 g (8 oz) pasta twists or other pasta shapes

1 head broccoli or ¼ cauliflower

1 red pepper, cored, deseeded and cut into small strips

425 g (14 oz) can pineapple pieces or rings, drained and cut into bite-sized pieces

125 g (4 oz) cooked ham in one slice, diced

Dressing:

25 g (1 oz) fresh coriander (stems and leaves) or a mixture of parsley and mint

4 tablespoons olive oil

1 tablespoon white wine vinegar or cider vinegar

salt and pepper

Cook the pasta shapes in plenty of boiling salted water for 10–12 minutes, or according to the packet instructions, until al dente. Drain, rinse thoroughly with cold water and drain well.

Slice the broccoli or cauliflower stem finely and separate the florets. Cook the sliced stem in boiling, salted water for 2 minutes. Add the florets and cook for 2 minutes. Drain well, refresh in cold water and drain again.

Make the dressing: purée the

uncovered, for 10–12 minutes or according to the packet instructions, stirring occasionally, until al dente.

Drain the pasta and refresh it briefly under cold running water to prevent overcooking. Drain it again well and leave to cool.

Meanwhile, make the mayonnaise. Beat together the egg yolk and mustard in a bowl, and season to taste with salt and pepper. Beat in the oil a drop at a time until the mixture emulsifies, then add the oil more quickly, in a thin steady stream. Thin down the mayonnaise with the tarragon vinegar. Add the tarragon, cover the bowl and set aside.

Mix together the pasta, chicken and prawns in a bowl. Halve the avocado lengthways and remove the stone and skin. Slice the flesh thinly and gently fold it into the salad. Cover the bowl tightly and chill in the refrigerator for 30 minutes.

To serve the salad, line a serving dish with lettuce leaves. Place the salad into the dish and spoon over the mayonnaise. Garnish with sprigs of tarragon.

Serves 4

---

left: four seasons pasta salad
right: pasta, cucumber and radish salad

Pasta, Cucumber and Radish Salad

125 g (4 oz) pasta shapes, such as
   shells, bows or spirals
175 g (6 oz) radishes sliced
½ cucumber, about 250 g (8 oz),
   diced
150 ml (5 fl oz) soured cream
salt and pepper
1 Cos lettuce, separated into leaves,
   to serve
2 spring onions, finely chopped, to
   garnish

Put the pasta into a large pan of boiling salted water. Bring back to the boil and cook for 10–12 minutes, or according to the packet instructions, until al dente. Rinse under cold water and drain.

Put the radishes and cucumber in a bowl and add the pasta. Stir in the soured cream, adding plenty of pepper and a little salt. Turn the pasta, radishes and cucumber over in the cream to coat thoroughly.

Arrange the lettuce leaves on a serving dish and spoon the salad into them. Garnish with the chopped spring onions.

Serves 4

Salami, Walnut and Pasta Salad

125 g (4 oz) short-cut wholewheat macaroni

250 g (8 oz) new potatoes, scrubbed but not scraped

125 ml (4 fl oz) vinaigrette dressing

3 spring onions, sliced

3 tablespoons walnut halves

125 g (4 oz) salami, skinned and diced

125 g (4 oz) coarse garlic sausage, skinned and diced

1 tablespoon chopped chives

6 tablespoons soured cream

1 teaspoon prepared mustard

salt and pepper

Cook the macaroni in boiling salted water for 10–12 minutes, or according to the packet instructions, until al dente. Drain it thoroughly.

At the same time, cook the potatoes in boiling salted water until they are just tender. Drain the potatoes and, as soon as they are cool enough to handle, rub off the skins. Dice or quarter the potatoes if they are large. While the pasta and potatoes are still hot, toss them in the vinaigrette dressing. Set this aside to cool. When the pasta and potatoes are cool, stir in the spring onions, walnuts (reserving a few of them for the garnish), salami, garlic sausage and chives.

Stir together the soured cream and mustard and add plenty of pepper. Spoon the dressing on to the salad, and toss to coat it thoroughly.

Arrange the salad on a serving platter and garnish with the reserved walnuts.

Serves 4

Salami Pasta Salad

125 g (4 oz) pasta bows or twists

125 g (4 oz) salami, derinded and chopped

200 g (7 oz) can sweetcorn, drained

3 celery sticks, chopped

12 green or black olives

1 small red pepper, cored, deseeded and chopped

1 tablespoon chopped parsley

1 tablespoon chopped basil

Dressing:

3 tablespoons vegetable oil

1 tablespoon lemon juice

pepper

Cook the pasta in boiling salted water for 10–12 minutes, or according to the packet instructions, until al dente. Drain, rinse under cold water, then drain again.

Allow the pasta to cool, then combine with the remaining salad ingredients in a large salad bowl.

Place the ingredients for the dressing in a screw-top jar, season with salt and pepper to taste, and shake vigorously until blended.

Pour the dressing over the salad and toss well to coat all the ingredients. Cover with clingfilm and chill until ready to serve. Toss again just before serving.

Serves 4

left: salami, walnut and pasta salad
right: pasta and pepper salad

Pasta and Pepper Salad

250 g (8 oz) small pasta shells

125 ml (4 fl oz) olive oil

½ garlic clove, crushed

handful of fresh basil leaves, chopped, or 1 tablespoon dried basil

50–75 g (2–3 oz) Parmesan cheese, freshly grated

4–6 tablespoons cider or white wine vinegar

3 small peppers (red, green and yellow, if possible), cored, deseeded and diced

salt and pepper

Cook the pasta in plenty of boiling salted water for 10–12 minutes, or according to the packet instructions, until al dente. Drain well, cool under cold running water, drain again and toss until dry in a tea towel.

Beat together the oil, garlic, basil and Parmesan. Stir in the vinegar and salt and pepper to taste.

Place the pasta in a large salad bowl, add the dressing and toss well. Chill, covered, until you are ready to serve.

Just before serving, add the peppers and toss again lightly to mix.

Serves 6

Roman Salad

250 g (8 oz) fresh tagliatelle verde
4 tablespoons Italian extra virgin
 olive oil
1 tablespoon white wine vinegar
4 spring onions, finely chopped
4 small, firm ripe tomatoes, skinned
 and diced
200 g (7 oz) can tuna, drained and
 flaked
50 g (2 oz) can anchovies in oil,
 drained and roughly chopped
25 g (1 oz) parsley, finely chopped
4 hard-boiled eggs, shelled
salt and pepper

Bring a large saucepan of salted
water to the boil. Add the
tagliatelle, stir and bring back to the
boil. Reduce the heat and boil,
uncovered, for 2–3 minutes
or according to the packet
instructions, stirring occasionally,
until al dente. Meanwhile, whisk
together the oil and vinegar in the
bottom of a large bowl.

Drain the tagliatelle and refresh it
briefly under cold running water to
prevent overcooking. Drain it again
well and transfer it to the bowl. Toss
the pasta with the dressing and
season with salt and pepper to taste.
Leave to cool, stirring occasionally.

When the pasta is cold, add the
spring onions, tomatoes, tuna,
anchovies and parsley. Halve the
eggs. Remove the yolks and set
them aside. Chop the whites finely
and add them to the salad. Fold the
salad ingredients together gently.

Cover the bowl tightly and place
it in the refrigerator to chill for
1–2 hours to allow the flavours to
mature and mingle. Sieve the
reserved egg yolks.

Before serving, fold the salad
ingredients together again. Adjust
the seasoning if necessary and
transfer to a serving bowl. Sprinkle
the sieved egg yolks on top and
serve chilled. Serve as a starter, or as
a side salad to accompany meat
or poultry.

Serves 4–6

Tagliatelle, Sausage and Butter Bean Salad

250 g (8 oz) tagliatelle verde
250 g (8 oz) Frankfurter sausages
375 g (12 oz) tomatoes
125 g (4 oz) butter beans, soaked and
 cooked, or 425 g (14 oz) can butter
 beans, drained
3 boxes cress
4 tablespoons olive oil
2 tablespoons white wine vinegar
1 teaspoon German mustard
1 garlic clove, crushed
salt and pepper

Cook the tagliatelle in boiling salted
water for 5 minutes, or according
to the packet instructions, until

al dente. Drain it, run cold water
through it and drain again. Cool
completely.

Thinly slice the sausages. Scald,
skin and chop the tomatoes.
Combine these with the tagliatelle
and beans. Cut in the cress. Beat the
remaining ingredients together to
make the dressing, season and fold
it into the salad.

Serves 4

Smoked Haddock Salad with Watercress Mayonnaise

1 kg (2 lb) smoked haddock
600 ml (1 pint) milk
1 small onion, peeled but left whole
2 cloves
large bunch of watercress, washed
 and stems discarded
250 ml (8 fl oz) mayonnaise
2 tablespoons natural yogurt
1 teaspoon paprika
2 bulbs fennel, finely shredded, leaves
 reserved
500 g (1 lb) tagliatelle verde
12 tablespoons olive oil
2 hard-boiled eggs, shelled
salt and pepper

Rinse the haddock, put in a shallow
dish and cover with boiling water.
Leave for 2 minutes, then drain and

refresh under cold water. Put into a large pan, pour in the milk and add water until the fish is just covered. Add the onion, studded with the cloves, and bring to the boil. Simmer for 20–25 minutes.

Drain the fish (reserving the milk for soup). Remove the skin and as many bones as possible, then flake into bite-sized pieces.

Take half the watercress and either chop finely in a food processor, or chop by hand, then pound lightly in a pestle and mortar. Mix the chopped watercress into the mayonnaise and stir in the yogurt, paprika and some pepper.

Mix the haddock into the mayonnaise, then fold in the shredded fennel. Taste the mixture, adding a little salt if necessary.

Meanwhile, cook the tagliatelle in boiling salted water for 5 minutes, or according to the packet instructions, until al dente. Drain well and stir in half the olive oil. Tip the noodles on to a serving dish, then add the haddock mayonnaise.

Arrange the remaining watercress on the fish, then halve the boiled eggs and remove the yolks. Crumble the yolks lightly, cut the whites into strips and sprinkle both over the fish. Serve at room temperature, lightly dressed with the remaining olive oil. Garnish with the reserved fennel leaves.

Serves 6

below: smoked haddock salad with watercress mayonnaise

Egg and Cheese

Macaroni Eggs Lyonnaise

250 g (8 oz) short-cut macaroni
25 g (1 oz) butter
1 tablespoon plain flour
300 ml (½ pint) milk
4 hard-boiled eggs, chopped
1 large onion, sliced
1 tablespoon oil
75 g (3 oz) Cheddar cheese, grated
salt and pepper

Cook the macaroni in plenty of boiling salted water for 8–10 minutes, or according to the packet instructions, until al dente.

Meanwhile, make the white sauce. Melt the butter in a pan, stir in the flour and cook for 30 seconds. Remove the pan from the heat and gradually stir in the milk. Cook over a gentle heat until thickened. Stir in the chopped hard-boiled eggs and season with salt and pepper to taste.

Drain the cooked macaroni and add to the sauce. Spoon into a lightly oiled ovenproof dish. Fry the sliced onion in a little oil until it starts to brown. Spoon the onion over the macaroni and sprinkle with the cheese. Bake in a preheated oven, 200°C (400°F), Gas Mark 6, for 15 minutes. Serve immediately with a tomato salad, if liked.

Serves 4

Trenette with Mixed Herbs and Pine Kernels

50–65 g (2–2½ oz) mixed herbs, such
   as basil, parsley and sage
50 g (2 oz) pine kernels
2 garlic cloves, roughly chopped
100 ml (3½ fl oz) olive oil
250–300 g (8–10 oz) dried trenette
4 tablespoons freshly grated Pecorino
   or Parmesan cheese
salt and pepper

Wash the herbs and pat them thoroughly dry with kitchen paper. Place them in a food processor. Add the pine kernels and garlic and chop very finely. Add the oil in a thin, steady stream, working until you obtain a fine, creamy sauce.

Bring a saucepan of salted water to the boil. Add the pasta, stir and bring back to the boil. Reduce the heat slightly and boil, uncovered, for 5 minutes, or according to the packet instructions, until al dente. Transfer the sauce to a warm bowl. Add the cheese and season with salt and pepper to taste. Stir well to blend. Drain the pasta. Add to the sauce and toss well to combine. Serve at once.

Serves 4

Cheese Pasta Soufflés

50 g (2 oz) small pasta shells
Sauce:
50 g (2 oz) butter or margarine
50 g (2 oz) plain flour
300 ml (½ pint) milk
¼ teaspoon dry mustard
75 g (3 oz) mature Cheddar cheese, grated
4 tablespoons grated Parmesan cheese
3 egg yolks
4 egg whites
salt and pepper

Cook the pasta shells in plenty of boiling salted water for 8–10 minutes, or according to the packet instructions, until al dente.

Drain the pasta, rinse with hot water and then drain thoroughly in a sieve.

To make the sauce, melt the butter or margarine in a saucepan, add the flour and cook for 1 minute. Gradually add the milk, off the heat, beating all the time. Bring to the boil, stirring, over a moderate heat and cook for 1 minute. Stir in the mustard, salt and pepper, Cheddar cheese, 2 tablespoons of the Parmesan and egg yolks, and beat together well.

Whisk the egg whites until stiff, add to the sauce with the pasta shells and fold in carefully until evenly mixed. Divide the mixture between 6 individual soufflé dishes or place in one large dish, each buttered and sprinkled with a little Parmesan cheese.

Cook in the centre of a preheated oven, 180°C (350°F), Gas Mark 4, for 25–30 minutes for the small soufflés or 40–45 minutes for the large soufflé. Serve immediately.

Serves 6

Variation:
Replace half of the Cheddar cheese with chopped ham or mushrooms and try wholewheat pasta.

left: macaroni eggs Lyonnaise
above: cheese pasta soufflés

Tagliatelle with Dolcelatte Cheese Sauce

25 g (1 oz) butter
175 g (6 oz) Dolcelatte cheese, rind
   removed, diced
150 ml (¼ pint) double cream
2 teaspoons finely chopped sage
250–300 g (8–10 oz) fresh tagliatelle
salt and pepper
sage sprigs, to garnish

Melt the butter in a heavy saucepan. Add the cheese and place the pan over a very low heat until the cheese has melted. Gradually stir in the cream, beating vigorously with a wooden spoon so that it blends into the cheese. Remove the pan from the heat, stir in the sage and cover.

Bring a large pan of salted water to the boil. Add the tagliatelle, stir and bring back to the boil. Reduce the heat slightly and boil, uncovered, for 3–4 minutes, or according to the packet instructions, until al dente.

Just before the pasta is ready, reheat the sauce and season with the pepper.

Drain the tagliatelle well and divide it equally between 4 warmed soup plates. Pour the sauce over the pasta and garnish with sage.

Serves 4

Pasta Alfredo

250–300 g (8–10 oz) fresh tagliatelle
25 g (1 oz) butter
150 ml (¼ pint) double cream
2 tablespoons finely chopped parsley
3 tablespoons freshly grated
   Parmesan cheese
salt and pepper

Bring a large saucepan of salted water to the boil. Add the pasta, stir and bring back to the boil. Reduce the heat slightly and boil, uncovered, for 3–4 minutes, or according to the packet instructions, stirring occasionally, until al dente.

Meanwhile, melt the butter in a small, heavy saucepan. Add the cream and parsley and heat through, stirring. Add the Parmesan with salt and pepper to taste and stir until the cheese has totally melted into the cream.

Drain the tagliatelle well and turn it into a warmed serving bowl. Pour over the sauce and toss lightly together. Serve at once, with extra cheese served separately, if liked. No accompaniment is necessary, apart from a bottle of dry white wine.

Serves 4

Spaghetti Carbonara

375 g (12 oz) spaghetti
175 g (6 oz) streaky bacon rashers,
   cut into strips
3 eggs
2 tablespoons single cream
40 g (1½ oz) Parmesan or Pecorino
   cheese, grated
40 g (1½ oz) butter
salt and pepper

Cook the spaghetti in plenty of boiling salted water for 8–10 minutes, or according to the packet instructions, until al dente. Drain the spaghetti, rinse with hot water and drain thoroughly in a sieve.

Fry the bacon gently in a frying pan until crisp and golden. Beat the eggs with the cream and cheese, and season with salt and pepper.

Melt the butter in a large saucepan, add the egg mixture and stir over a moderate heat until just beginning to thicken. Add the fried bacon and the spaghetti quickly, and toss lightly together. Serve immediately.

Serves 4

right: spaghetti carbonara

Pour the tomato sauce evenly over the cannelloni, ensuring they are all covered. Sprinkle with the remaining Parmesan cheese.

Bake in a preheated oven, 180°C (350°F), Gas Mark 4, for 35–40 minutes, until the cannelloni are tender (test by piercing with a sharp pointed knife). Serve hot, garnished with fresh herb sprigs and celery leaves, if liked.

Serves 3–4

Ricotta and Spinach Cannelloni

250 g (8 oz) fresh spinach, washed

125 g (4 oz) Ricotta cheese

3 tablespoons grated Parmesan cheese

2 pinches of grated nutmeg

1 egg yolk

1 tablespoon chopped fresh mixed herbs, such as marjoram, chives, parsley and chervil

6–8 cannelloni tubes

salt and pepper

Tomato sauce:

500 g (1 lb) ripe tomatoes, skinned and chopped

1 small onion, chopped

1 celery stick, chopped

1 tablespoon tomato purée

½ teaspoon sugar

To garnish (optional):
fresh herb sprigs
celery leaves

Put the spinach in a saucepan with just the water that clings to it after washing. Cover and cook for 5–7 minutes, shaking the pan occasionally, until the spinach wilts. Drain well and chop finely.

Place the spinach in a bowl with the Ricotta cheese, 1 tablespoon of the Parmesan cheese, the nutmeg, egg yolk, herbs, and salt and pepper to taste. Mix well.

Carefully fill the cannelloni tubes with the spinach mixture, using a small teaspoon. Place in a buttered shallow ovenproof dish in one layer.

Place all the sauce ingredients in a saucepan. Bring to the boil, reduce the heat and cook for 20 minutes. If liked, press through a sieve or purée in a blender or food processor until fairly smooth.

Fettuccine in Four Cheeses

500 g (1 lb) dried fettuccine

1 onion

2 garlic cloves

Sauce:

25 g (1 oz) butter

2 garlic cloves, sliced

50 g (2 oz) each Emmental, Mozzarella, Parmesan and Cheddar, grated

175 ml (6 fl oz) single cream

salt and pepper

To garnish:

1 tablespoon chopped parsley

1 tablespoon chopped basil

Place the pasta, onion and garlic in a large pan of boiling salted water and cook for 5 minutes, or according to the packet instructions, until al dente.

Meanwhile, make the sauce. Melt the butter in a pan, add the garlic and cook, without browning, for 3 minutes. Stir in the cheeses and cream and continue stirring over a low heat until the cheeses have melted. Season with salt and pepper to taste.

Drain the pasta and remove the onion and garlic. Toss the pasta in the sauce, sprinkle with the herbs and serve immediately, with a tomato and onion salad.

Serves 4

*left: ricotta and spinach cannelloni
below: wholewheat pasta with broccoli and blue cheese*

Wholewheat Pasta with Broccoli and Blue Cheese

75 g (3 oz) wholewheat pasta shells
125 g (4 oz) broccoli, cut into small florets
50 g (2 oz) blue cheese
25 g (1 oz) butter
50 ml (2 fl oz) double or whipping cream
salt and pepper

Cook the pasta in plenty of boiling salted water for 5 minutes, or according to the packet instructions, until al dente. Add the broccoli and cook for a further 3 minutes. Drain well and remove the pasta and broccoli from the pan.

Put the pan back on the heat and add the blue cheese, butter and cream to the pan. Heat gently, stirring all the time to make a smooth sauce. Taste and adjust the seasoning carefully as blue cheese can sometimes be quite salty. Return the pasta and broccoli to the pan. Toss to mix thoroughly with the sauce and heat through gently. Serve immediately on a warmed plate.

Serves 2

Index